the toilet
seat

the toilet seat

LATHA

HARPER
NON-FICTION

First published in English by Notion Press 2017
Published in India by Harper Non-Fiction 2025
An imprint of HarperCollins *Publishers*
HarperCollins *Publishers* India, Cyber City, Building 10-A, Gurugram,
Haryana – 122002, India
www.harpercollins.co.in

2 4 6 8 10 9 7 5 3 1

Copyright © Latha Balasubramanian 2017, 2025

P-ISBN: 978-93-6989-252-5
E-ISBN: 978-93-6989-379-9

Latha Balasubramanian asserts the moral right
to be identified as the author of this work.

The views and opinions expressed in this book are the author's own and the facts are as reported by her, and the publishers are not in any way liable for the same. This book discusses themes of love, sex, heartbreak and coping, including mentions of self-harm and harmful actions. The content of this book should not replace consultation with your doctor or qualified mental health specialists for anyone experiencing anxiety, depression, suicidal ideation, or any other emotional or mental health concerns. The author and the publisher disclaim any liability or responsibility to any person or entity for any loss, damage, injury, or expense that may arise from the use of any content in this book. Any use of, or reliance on, information in this book is solely the responsibility of the reader.

All rights reserved. No part of this publication may be reproduced, stored in a retrieval system, or transmitted, in any form or by any means, electronic, mechanical, photocopying, recording or otherwise, without the prior permission of the publishers.

Without limiting the exclusive rights of any author, contributor or the publisher of this publication, any unauthorized use of this publication to train generative artificial intelligence (AI) technologies is expressly prohibited. HarperCollins also exercise their rights under Article 4(3) of the Digital Single Market Directive 2019/790 and expressly reserve this publication from the text and data-mining exception.

Typeset in 12.5/16.2 Bembo Std at
HarperCollins *Publishers* India

Printed and bound at
Replika Press Pvt. Ltd.

This book is produced from independently certified FSC® paper to
ensure responsible forest management.

HarperCollins Publishers, Macken House, 39/40 Mayor Street Upper,
Dublin 1, D01 C9W8, Ireland

To the society that raised me.

'If you don't laugh during sex at least once,
you are having sex with the wrong person.'
— **Extramadness.com**

'It takes more than sex to build a great marriage,
but it is nearly impossible to build a great marriage
without it!'
— **Davewilliams.org**

'If sex isn't an important part of your
marriage, you can't beef if your wife or
husband does this unimportant thing with
somebody else every once in a while,
if you have no interest in it.'
— **Dan Savage**

CONTENTS

Prologue ix

1. The Basic Necessities of Life 1
2. The Dirty Word 4
3. Repercussions of Treating Sex as a Taboo or a Dirty Word 9
4. Women and Society 17
5. Union of Mind and Body 24
6. Secrecy, Suppression and Education 27
7. The Toilet Seat 33
8. Sex as an Expression of Love 47
9. Extramarital Affairs 55
10. Going Beyond Trust 73
11. Friendship as the Basis of a Relationship 77

12.	Desperation	81
13.	Masturbation	85
14.	The Institution Called Marriage	91
15.	Marriage and Family	99
16.	Possessiveness	107
17.	Complementing Each Other	111
18.	Driving Away Inhibitions	117
19.	Male Ego	121
20.	Health and Sex Education	123
21.	Food and Sex	126
22.	Loss of Interest in Sex in Women	129
23.	Value Systems	132
24.	Rules for a Good Relationship	137
25.	A Glimpse into Married Life	143
26.	Child's Play	147
27.	Myths about Love and Sex	150
28.	A Conformist View	153
29.	Need of the Hour and Hope for the Future	159

Addenda (*Afterthoughts that cropped up after the first edition of the book*)

30.	Is There an Upper Age Limit for Sex?	165
31.	Role of Parents in Child Sexual Abuse	169

Acknowledgements 175

PROLOGUE

We don't think too much about sex; we're merely thinking about it in the wrong way.
— Alain de Botton

THIS BOOK IS NOT AIMED AT PROVIDING solutions to facilitate having good sex or an enjoyable life. It is also not a research-based treatise on sex. Instead, it is an attempt at a critical analysis of the way sex is generally perceived and practised, and of the social stigma that is attached to the very word.

The subject of sex has always been an intriguing one for me. I am sure it is so for many of us, because anything that has a taboo attached to it, creates an interest in us. Anything that is forbidden and suppressed, builds our curiosity and urges us to know more about it, experience more of it.

Many people have written about sex. In fact, I have read quite a few books on the subject. These books either talk about the physical act of sex or they deal with sex through a physiological, philosophical or psychological lens. I would encourage you to first read books of the latter kind, as it is not possible to enjoy lasting pleasure without understanding the real depth of the emotions connected with sex.

So, what is it that I am trying to do here in this book? I am just trying to examine and understand sex in a very straightforward way, and I am basing my analysis on what I have perceived through my experiences, observed in my surroundings and heard of from others. In my opinion, simple, basic things like love and sex have been clothed in unnecessary complexities, creating havoc in our lives and society.

Like most of us, I too grew up in a family where sex was never discussed. I have never seen any physical intimacy between my mother and father, or any of the married couples among my relatives, neighbours or friends. Incidentally, my first brush with sex coincided with the first movie I ever watched in my life. An uncle from my neighbourhood, older than my father, took his youngest son (who was ten years old), my brother (who was nine) and me (eight years) to a Tamil movie about Lord Murugan (a deity worshipped mostly by Tamilians, and fondly called Thamizh Kadavul). During the interval, I felt like peeing. Uncle, however, made me wait until the movie resumed playing after the interval and then took me to the men's toilet. Once I finished, he pulled out his penis and asked me to hold it tightly for a while. I could not think straight; I did not know how to respond. I just obediently did what he asked me to do and then came out of the men's toilet. From what I can remember about it now, although I felt awkward about what had happened, I was not actually bothered by it. However, I stopped going to this uncle's house after that.

Then there was another incident, involving another neighbour who was studying in a law college and was living alone. My brother and I used to call him anna (brother). One day, he fell ill and my parents gave me some food to deliver to him. When I went to his room, anna pulled me on to his bed forcefully. Then, despite my protests, he squeezed my tiny breasts so hard that they started hurting. He held my palm tight around his penis and pulled it up, down, up, down. The sticky liquid that rushed out onto my palm from his penis that day still stinks in my memory.

I am not going to narrate every single incident of molestation that I went through at an age when I had not even heard the word 'sex'. As I grew up, I started to understand that children of both sexes and women of all ages (from little babies to the old and withered) are subjected to molestation, rape and torture not just at the hands of strangers, but also by people who are respected at large and who have a good reputation in society.

As for me, I experienced a major heartbreak at the age of fourteen when I had to go through the same horror with my father. This time, the abuse went on for almost two years until I ran away from home, only to be brought back the same evening and beaten up.

Much later, I noticed an irony in all these incidents (and I hope you noticed it too). Someone who was clearly quite religious and god-fearing took me to watch a movie about a deity and then did something dirty to me. A person whom I addressed as anna, forcefully used my hands to ejaculate, even though we've all been told from childhood that a brother is someone who is protective of us and whom we must always respect. And lastly, my father, the man who was the reason for my very existence on earth, who was supposed to protect me at all times, did filthy things to me.

Even now, I find people coming to me for sex, citing so many reasons. But I find most of their reasons very stupid, mainly because their true intentions are very clear—they simply want a 'yes' from me, an agreement that I will sleep with them.

PROLOGUE

Many of these men approach me under the pretext of 'love'. Some of them say that they don't enjoy sex with their wives, either because their wives are not interested in sex or because they don't get along well with them. While I call the former hypocrites, the latter clearly puzzle me. Are women supposed to take pity on these 'deprived' men and have sex with them as an act of charity? It also surprises me that while a man's ego does not allow him to accept a 'no' from a woman, in trying to save his ego, he does not seem to mind losing his self-respect.

Very rarely do I come across men who tell me directly, and in as many words, that they would like to have sex with me. Irrespective of whether I accept the invitation or not, I would, and certainly do, appreciate these men for their straightforwardness.

A few of my male friends have told me that there are some women who are like the men I have talked about in the previous paragraphs. I guess that is true. The urge and the desperation to have sex are equal in both genders. I have read newspaper articles about the molestation of teenage boys by women, the so-called 'aunties', who are considered to be good neighbours or caring relatives.

But, because I am a woman and because this book is a result of my experiences, it may seem like I am blaming the other gender. That, however, is not my intention. My intention is to analyse the causes and effects of maintaining secrecy around sex, of looking at it as a tabooed topic to discuss and of regarding premarital sex as a sin.

I've always wondered what we are boasting about when we talk of our 'rich culture'. We talk about monogamy, we talk about family values, we talk a lot about the sentiments of fathers and mothers, and we talk endlessly about the countless gods in our pantheon. But a culture can be appreciated only when there is harmony and mutual respect for fellow human beings. And family values? In most instances, the members of a family don't seem to be bothered about each other's welfare. In the name of family and values, most people seem to live a hypocritical life. If what we boast about is really true, then why is there so much desperation, and the resultant perversion, among people seeking sex? Where is the problem? Clearly, this is a deep-rooted issue which needs to be sorted out urgently.

Before I get on with the main chapters of this book, I would like to make it very clear that whatever has been written in the pages ahead does not in any way single out an individual or a particular gender. This book is based on the people I have met, the men and the women I have come across in my life. And while I am not saying that there are no exceptions, I am also saying that there is no rule either.

However, the fact remains that ours is a male-dominated society and women have been the suppressed lot for many generations. Despite this truth, as far as possible, I have tried to analyse everything from the perspective of both genders, and I request you to read this book without any bias towards any particular gender.

Why This Title?

You may wonder why this book is called *The Toilet Seat* and what exactly does a toilet seat have to do with sex? Well, you will discover this connection as you make your way through the book.

1

The Basic Necessities of Life

WE'VE ALWAYS BEEN TOLD THAT THE BASIC necessities of life are three in number: Food, clothing and shelter. But I would say that they are, in fact, four in number: Food, sex, shelter and clothing, in the exact order of priority in which they have been written. In fact, if we think about this a little more, we will realize that the basic necessities of life for early man would've been only food and sex, and then, maybe, shelter. The need for food and sex is created by our instincts; even animals, whose lives are guided purely by their instincts, crave for food and sex. The requirement for shelter, on the other hand, could've been driven by challenging climatic and environmental conditions that early man must have faced. Similarly, clothing is a mark of civilization and it would not have been a basic necessity of life for early man.

Even people who go without food do not deprive themselves of sex, such is the force and allure of sexual energy. Early man must have gone around eating anything and everything to survive, and would have had sex with anyone and everyone for the sake of pleasure. Only after enjoying this pleasure would he have even known that sex is also the way to reproduce. He would've perhaps experienced the pleasures of sex much earlier than the taste of food.

We have come a long way from those jungle days into the world of civilization and refined tastes. Today, food, for example, is not just a means for survival. Food is also about satisfying our taste buds and, in the process of doing so, it helps us survive. Shelter and clothing too have evolved over the ages.

However, the same cannot be said about sex. We have pushed sex into a dark room, locked it up tightly and built an electric fence around it. We call it a 'sin' when two individuals have sex without the approval of society, which is actually a non-entity in the whole equation between the two individuals. Until society gives its approval in the form of 'marriage' and grants sex a sanctimonious status, it is kept under wraps.

All of this makes me wonder why, when the taste of the food we consume has taken such a dominant place in our lives, the pleasure of sex is being treated differently. This differential treatment has resulted in sex occupying a predominant but furtive place in the minds of people, causing perversions in thoughts and actions.

2

The Dirty Word

IF MY PARENTS HAD NOT HAD SEX, I WOULD NOT be here today talking about this 'dirty' word. You too would not be here, reading this book, had it not been for the act of sex. If sex is indeed dirty, then why are we taught to respect our parents who had sex in the process of having us?

When marriage and childbirth are considered sacred, how come sex is a DIRTY word?

Elements such as water, fire and air are the essence of life. By themselves, they are pure in nature; they cannot lose their inherent purity on their own. But *we* can contaminate them and then call them 'impure'. And we have done just that. Human beings have taken it upon themselves to contaminate everything that is pure in nature, everything that makes the world go around, everything that supports their existence, adds beauty to their surroundings and brings life to their existence. And sex is no exception!

Sex is not dirty by itself. But sex becomes dirty when it is forced upon another person through emotional or physical threats. This can happen in the sex trade, this can happen at large in a public place, and this can also happen within the supposedly sacred institutions of marriage and family.

Sex has been made dirty by man because of the secrecy and suppression surrounding it, because of the restrictions imposed on it in the form of social norms and customs, and because of the injustice meted out to women by society. Sex, instead of being a medium of sharing and expressing love, has become a weapon used against each other. Man is mostly on top and it is, therefore, easy for him to crush the woman below him. Of course, in some situations, the woman too has the power to crush a man and strip him off his dignity, wealth and what not! I can say one thing for sure. It is a widely held notion that 'good', 'decent' people don't talk about sex openly and only 'dirty' people talk about sex.

I had a friend once. We used to talk candidly about many issues, both general and personal in nature. Whenever I wanted to pour my heart out, I could count on him to just sit and listen to me. Most of the times though, when we talk about our problems with others, they think that we expect them to sort out our issues. Not at all!

Sometimes, we just want to share our feelings and problems. We are not always looking for a solution to be offered to us. When we share our feelings with others, we feel relieved and lighter. We might even become more energetic and level-headed about facing the problem and resolving it on our own. This friend was one such person for me. I could share anything with him. However, one day, the topic of our discussion somehow veered towards sex and, as always, we shared our views on it.

That same night, my friend called me and asked, 'Will you have sex with me?' I was taken aback. I could not understand what had led him to ask me that question; what had gone wrong? He told me that he had never seen me in 'that sense' till then, but when we discussed the subject of sex so openly, he could not help but imagine having sex with me. He said he had called me because he could not think of anything else and that he had become very desperate to have sex with me. When I told him that sex was just another subject of discussion and that I was not interested in having sex with him, he asked me many questions, including 'Why not?' I said that sex had to be a mutual want, a spontaneous desire, and, in this case, I did not feel like having sex with him. So, I refused him firmly. He accused me of having planted the seed in his head by initiating the conversation about sex. He said that since he had now started looking at me differently, he could not continue our friendship. From then on, he stopped communicating with me. I have no hard feelings towards him, but I feel sad that a simple discussion about sex sounded the deathknell on a good friendship.

Love and sex are natural feelings that arise organically in us, without anyone forcibly inducing them. So why do people feel hurt and humiliated when someone they are attracted to or want to have sex with does not reciprocate those feelings? Why do they take such a refusal personally? I cannot force myself to love someone or enjoy sex with them. Sex and love are like people's tastes in food—they vary from person to person. Can we question this basic truth?

There is, however, almost always a confusion between love and sex. The physical arousal to have sex is often misunderstood as love and we use the term 'love' to make others have sex with us. Then there is the fear factor that prevents us from expressing ourselves clearly. So scared are we of being misunderstood that even if we genuinely like someone and want to spend the rest of our life with that someone, we don't know how to approach the other person and confess our feelings.

Ours is a country where people like Vatsyayana lived and wrote the *Kamasutra*, where sculptures depicting sexual postures were carved, temples like Khajuraho were built and several scriptures that talked about sex among other things, were written. But today, we all seem to have become closeted. We've lost that open culture and come far, far away from nature.

If sex is taught and talked about openly, we will definitely be able to reduce the instances of rape, abuse and molestation that plague our society, and save our future generations from physical and mental torture. This openness can strengthen the relationship between sexual partners, make sex more enjoyable and also help healthier friendships blossom between people of the opposite gender. Only then will sex no longer be considered a 'dirty' word.

3

Repercussions of Treating Sex as a Taboo or a Dirty Word

Obsession

IT IS THE BASIC PSYCHOLOGY OF THE HUMAN MIND to be obsessed with something that it cannot get or know about easily. The curious mind will never keep quiet until it learns what has been withheld from it. If the mind does not learn this and if the body is not nurtured with what it needs, the mind becomes obsessed. When a child, for example, is still in the liquid and soft food stage, it often tries to grab what the adults are eating in front of it. We, as adults, know that the food we are eating is not good for the child since it cannot digest it. So, we explain to the child that the food is very spicy and try to make it understand through some animated actions since it cannot process language. Objectively speaking, this is much more difficult than talking to an adolescent about sex. Why, then, don't we engage in the easier act? Why do adults refrain from talking to teenagers about the biological changes happening in their bodies and the implications of these changes on their social, physical and psychological well-being? In fact, there's nothing wrong in getting them a good book on this subject so they can understand the changes they're going through. But how many parents do this?

We keep saying sex is bad and we keep suppressing the facts. But the more we suppress information, the more obsessed teenagers are going to get. With technological advancements, they have all the access to information. The problem is they tend to land on the wrong information. They just learn that sex is a pleasurable act. They don't learn anything else about its true nature. In this twisted scenario, every girl that a boy comes across becomes an object of sex in his mind, and every girl tries to attract a boy with her physical features and attributes. This is where the problem starts. When two people of the opposite sex (or it could be people of the same sex too) get attracted to each other physically or when they get into an exploratory mode with each other's bodies, they misunderstand their feelings as 'love'. This is one of the most common repercussions of suppressing knowledge about sex.

How long will this sort of attraction towards another person last? Till we get attracted to another 'body'? Till we have the opportunity to have sex with someone else? Most relationships break after a point in time, sometimes after wreaking great physical and emotional damage. If the man and the woman are somehow able to go ahead with the relationship and enter wedlock, they end up in a loveless marriage. I would like to repeat here that whatever I say need not hold good for everyone, but I think it holds good for a majority of the people.

The fact is, whether people indulge in sex or not, sex has taken a predominant place in almost everyone's mind.

The culmination of love should lead to sex. Love should happen first and then it should result in sex. However, in our society, sex happens first. Even our matrimonial system seems to advocate this. In arranged marriages, the sex happens before the couple has a chance to fall in love. Sometimes, love may not happen at all. And in the so-called love marriages, physical attraction is presumed to be love. By pushing away and hiding all knowledge about sex, we have demeaned the very meaning of love.

The Approach

Because of the widely held belief that sex is only about the body, people often do not connect with their partner's mind and heart when they indulge in sex. It becomes an entirely physical act that is done for the pleasure of the body.

When the required mental and emotional connections don't happen, we're not bothered about the sexual pleasure that our partner should also experience. We don't respect the other person's possession—their body. We do not know how enjoyable sex can be for both the mind and the body when the connections are complete. Even if we're concerned about the other person's enjoyment, we don't know what makes them happy. And on top of it all, we're in a state of urgency to relieve ourselves of the built-up tension in our nerves.

Even men who understand the importance of foreplay do it mechanically. They don't understand that foreplay is an act that should bring out their love, passion and respect for the person whose body they are dealing with. When we are sad or are mourning, someone holding our hands or putting their hands across our shoulders gives us warmth and strength, more so than what a hundred words of compassion can achieve. Words are mere words after all, whereas the touch of a person can clearly transmit energy. People should know that everything cannot be faked. There are some truths that can never be hidden.

When there is no connection, what can one really expect? One can only expect the worst results from what is clearly a bad approach. When we've not made any efforts to bring in the fire in the first place, why do we think the fire will simply stay on?

We crave for sexual fulfilment, but we don't attain it. So, quite naturally, we get obsessed with it. Even after entering into a marriage and having sex every day, we still crave for more sex, perhaps with someone else, all in the hope that our needs will be fulfilled. But most of us are conditioned by existing social norms and we choose to live with what we have. We resign ourselves to the fact that we are married to a particular person and that this is what we will get from him or her. Outwardly, we behave as if sex is not required, as if we are doing okay, but internally, we are starved.

Some bold people (although others may call them morally weak) seek satisfaction elsewhere. But there is no certainty that the new relationship will be sexually satisfactory either. And if that is indeed the case, then these bold ones carry the burden of guilt and the weight of another loveless relationship. As for the rare lucky ones who may find joy in a new relationship, they're constantly living with the fear of being caught.

Let me not unfairly assume that everyone is entering into an extramarital affair for sex. It's quite possible for people to fall in love outside their marriage as well, but I will deal with this later.

Manifestations of Perversion

Needless to say, an obsession with sex in the long-term causes perversions. (Here, I'm not talking about serious crimes like rape, gang rape, child rape and murder, which are rampant in our sick world.) Let us look at the manifestations of this perversion:

1. I'm sure many of you would've noticed that some men don't look into the eyes of the woman they are talking to. Their eyes are, instead, always fixed on the woman's breasts. I don't know if they realize that this causes a lot of embarrassment for the woman and hinders her capacity to have a normal conversation. These men may not mean any harm, but they still lose their credibility as decent men who respect women.
2. Whenever a woman is raped or molested, there are people (both men and women) who tend to

blame her for having brought it upon herself. Either she had dressed 'provocatively' or she had been out till very late in the night. There are some men who even try to rationalize the actions of a rapist. This is an extremely dangerous kind of perversion and it seems to suggest that they would've committed the crime themselves if they had the guts to do it. It wouldn't be an exaggeration to say that these kinds of people perhaps rape women in their minds day in and day out.

3. There are perverted, sex-starved men who brush their hands against a woman's nipples and push their protruding penis into her back in public places, using the crowds around as a cover.

4. Then there are those 'uncles' and 'aunties' who wait for an opportunity to grope the private parts of any adolescent or young child they come in contact with. In a conservative society like ours, people like these will always find convenient ways to exploit the innocence and vulnerability of children.

5. There are people who disregard others' privacy for the sake of their sexual satisfaction. They peep into bedrooms and bathrooms to look at people in the nude, or secretly watch someone having sex or taking a bath.

6. There are some people for whom watching porn is not a pastime but an unhealthy addiction.
7. Wet chats, not just between people who know and are intimate with each other but also with anyone and everyone, without even knowing whether the person at the other end is a man or a woman, is another form of perversion.

I am sure in a society where children are imparted sexual education at a particular age, treated equally, irrespective of the gender they belong to, allowed to play together, laugh together, grow up together and taught to understand the unity despite the physical differences, there will be less desperation and perversion, and the consent of the other person will become more important as there would be mutual respect between people.

4

Women and Society

Though things are changing slowly, our society is still a male-dominated one—and there are different rules for women and men, especially when it comes to the subject of sex.

For instance, while it is okay for men to talk about sex openly, women cannot. In fact, women don't even take the liberty of talking about it, because when they do decide to come out and express their views and perceptions, society considers them loose and immoral.

A woman who discusses sex candidly (that too just the basic stuff and not the deeper, more intimate details) is not expected to say 'no' to the advances of a man. The general perception is that if a woman talks about sex with a man or in front of a man, she will be willing to sleep with anyone and everyone. She is labelled as '*that* kind' of a woman. And if 'that kind' of a woman says no to a man, it hits his ego very badly. What people don't seem to understand is the difference between talking about sex and sexy talk.

I don't understand this hypocrisy. When I talk about food, I don't find a queue of men standing in front of my house with plates in their hands because they've assumed that I'll be offering them food. However, when I talk about sex, they don't think or assume—they simply go ahead and decide that I am inviting them to have sex with me.

If a woman refuses to sleep with a man, especially after talking to him about sex, all sorts of absurd questions are put forward to her. 'Then why did you talk about it at all?' she is asked. Or, 'I am sure you don't think it's wrong to sleep with other men. Then why don't you want to sleep with me?' Should the woman not buckle under the interrogation and, instead, continue to refuse the man, not only does the man's ego get deeply affected, but the woman is also blamed and negatively characterized for her openness.

But why should a woman who dares to talk about sex candidly be perceived as someone who is okay sleeping with anyone and everyone? Perhaps this is because women in our society have been told to 'behave' themselves properly at all times. So, a woman who talks freely about sex is a woman who is disobeying this rule and is, therefore, someone who will also freely sleep with anyone.

Our society also assumes that women don't approach men for sex. This is one of the reasons why a man keeps thrusting forward his wish to have sex with her even after a clear no. Men assume that a woman will say no to sex even if she wants to say yes because that's how she is supposed to behave and that his persistence will eventually bring out a yes from her.

Though this stance might appear absurd, it is also a fact that in our society, a woman is not supposed to accept a proposal easily as that would, in all likelihood, brand her as an immoral woman. But even if she is willing to have sex with people she likes, why should anyone assume that she would be willing to sleep with anyone and everyone who approaches her? What does love, sex or physical attraction mean to these people? And what is it that people want to achieve by forcing someone to have sex with them? I can keep adding questions here (in fact, it is questions like these that have paved the way for this book), but making the list any longer will not change anything.

Objectification of Women

Objectifying women is a very normal and acceptable thing in our society. Both men and women do this. Though a few of us see it as a despicable act, many women do not seem to mind it. I see this as a deep-rooted psychological manifestation of the way we bring up our girls.

In most Indian families, boys are dressed casually in jeans, shorts and T-shirts. 'You look like a prince, no matter what you wear,' is the general compliment that boys receive from their parents. In contrast, a lot of effort is put into prettying up girls. They are dressed in traditional clothes, adorned with fancy bindis, flowers and other accessories, and made to feel like princesses. They are told that their Prince Charming will appear one fine day and take them away, but only once they grow up to be beautiful.

This may seem like a very casual, harmless pattern of behaviour that parents and onlookers indulge in. However, deep down, we are planting a seed in the minds of young girls that they should always dress well enough to attract the attention of others, especially the opposite gender. They are unconsciously told that unless they doll up, they are not going to be considered beautiful. Thus, girls do not feel confident about themselves without the numerous external beautifying elements weighing them down. This is how we raise our girls. We unwittingly ingrain in them the belief that a woman's core objective in life is to appear beautiful to others. As girls step into adolescence, their focus is only on beautifying themselves because they've been told again and again that they must be beautiful in order to attract good-looking and smart men.

This need to look good in the eyes of others, especially men, only grows stronger through the years, and does not go down. I am no exception to this. So, the process and experience of objectification, especially self-objectification, begins here.

In a male-dominated society, where a few religions even believe that women are created solely for the pleasure and service of men, the objectification of women doesn't come as a surprise at all. In fact, when a woman protests about this, she is looked down upon as an alien.

Once, on a relaxed Sunday evening, I was reading a book when I heard my phone beep. It was a WhatsApp message. I took my eyes off the page I was on and picked up my mobile to look at the message. It was a picture of two big breasts painted in different colours, gift-wrapped with a ribbon knotted across them. To my complete shock, the message had been forwarded by a friend of mine whom I had always respected.

I literally went wild looking at it. I sent my friend a message back, saying, 'How can you send such a thing? I never expected this from you. I am really hurt.' His response to this appalled me to no end. He seemed to be surprised by my reaction. He replied, very irritatingly, 'What is wrong with you? Why do you have to react so strongly? I found it amusing and so I sent it to you. I don't see any reason for you to react like this. Maybe age is catching up with you, and you've lost your sense of humour and are becoming very sensitive.'

Here is why his response angered and also puzzled me. Should objectifying a woman's body ever be seen as a joke? Every day, we come across sexist, derogatory remarks being made by people around us. They act or say things in a very matter-of-fact manner. The jokes that are forwarded over WhatsApp and the messages that get posted on Facebook are all received without anyone raising a brow or batting an eyelid. Have we all become so immune to such demeaning behaviours that when someone raises an objection to such jokes, people wonder what is wrong with them?

This objectification extends to literature as well. If we analyse the work of Indian writers, especially poets, we can see that they have always described women as a flower or the moon, the earth and so on. A woman is generally not talked about as a human being and is always compared with objects, whereas a man is always a man, a human being.

These comparisons seem harmless when we look at them superficially. But they have unconsciously bred the belief that women are always meant for the use of men. As a result, when it comes to sex, a woman becomes an object in the eyes of the man. However, it is also true that women in our society don't seem to have any qualms about accepting this. Not only do they appear to not think too deeply about these issues, but they also don't voice their true emotions or feelings.

5

Union of Mind and Body

> *Sex is emotion in motion.*
>
> — Mae West

FOR SOME PEOPLE, SEX IS A UNION OF BODIES. FOR most others, however, it is nothing but a quick process of ejaculation. In my opinion, masturbation is a much better indulgence than loveless sex.

About 90 per cent of people do not think that sex is a union of both the body and the mind. I think that when people understand this, there is no way they will take the other person for granted, which is generally the case. But then who cares about love? Who cares about understanding the true essence of sex? I am sure the 'fast-sex' culture existed much before the fast-food culture came into the scene. Interestingly though, while we call pizzas and burgers 'fast food', we actually spend way more time consuming these fast foods than we do in our beds with the people we have sex with. That is why sex has degraded to a large extent. It has become a mundane process which ends with the man ejaculating. There are no loving words that are shared, no foreplay, no concern for the partner's involvement and enjoyment.

As Paulo Coelho says in his book *Eleven Minutes*:

> Anyone who is in love is making love the whole time, even when they're not. When two bodies meet, it is just the cup overflowing. They can stay together for hours, even days. They begin the dance one day and finish it the next, or—such is the pleasure they experience—they may never finish it. No eleven minutes for them.

Sex has been reduced to just a physical act and our society does not, in any way, help people understand that it is not so. By keeping sex in the dark and not allowing people to learn about it the proper way, we have allowed a distorted view of sex to take root. The general belief in our society is that as long as people are ejaculating and producing a kid or two, they are having sex and enjoying it too. This is merely an illusion.

Some time ago, I read these words somewhere and they resonated very strongly with me. And although I cannot recall who the author is, let me put them down here anyway:

> Sex without love is a meaningless experience. It is at the root of life and has to be understood fully to experience it. But there are stories where even very great men have fallen for sex from great heights to the shallows. True sex never fails as it is a bondage between two souls that have come together. Basically, it is not the sex that gives pleasure, but the true partner gives it. Therefore, sex can be termed as an art in itself, a kind of act that is good when properly enacted, but to enjoy it thoroughly, it also needs the cooperation of the mind as well with a clear heart and soul. Sex is not just an act of pleasure but the feeling of togetherness, being so close to another person and being comfortable in the partner. If love can be termed as the result of chemistry between two people, sex is nothing but an act of biology between them.

6

Secrecy, Suppression and Education

How many of us are ready to discuss sex in an open forum? I am not talking about male friends getting together and describing a woman's body, or women getting together and talking about what they did with their husbands, partners or boyfriends. I mean a healthy discussion on the nature of sex as such, and how it impacts our life and the sutras of it.

Our great ancestors have really enjoyed sex and they did not seem to have felt any shame about it. But through the years, sex has somehow turned into a thing of secrecy.

This is unfortunate because what we need is for parents, teachers and other responsible elders to teach youngsters about sex as soon as they reach adolescence. Won't they learn about it on their own when the time comes? This is a frequently asked counter question. But let me tell you something: Yes, youngsters do learn about sex on their own, but they learn it the wrong way from the outside world. Then again, 'when the time comes' is a very vague phrase. How do we know when the time actually strikes?

We teach our children so many things about life. Yet, we don't allow them to inquire and learn about themselves. We not only leave the topic of sex aside, but we also ensure that they do not learn anything about it till they get married. But the truth is that as soon as a child attains puberty (there is scientific proof that even a male child attains puberty at a certain age and has a menstruation cycle, just like a woman, though it is not obvious), sexual energy automatically starts flowing within him/her. In the absence of any scope of having an open conversation with their parents, children become quite confused about the physical changes happening within their bodies. This results in mental instability. When it comes to sex, specifically, youngsters become naturally curious about it and end up exploring it in an unhealthy way.

There are reports, for instance, of teenage boys raping small girls. There are boys who get molested and abused by adult men and women, and, in some cases, the boys end up becoming excited by such encounters; it becomes an obsession with them. There are so many adolescents who fall prey to the unexplored world of sex and lose their vision of the future. They end up entering exploitative, abusive relationships because the pent-up sexual energy and the curiosity inside them urged them to get physically close to the other person.

Some youngsters even think that they are in love. Complications and complexities become the order of their lives. But such incidents are not reported and not even talked about.

Keeping youngsters away from the knowledge of sex is a dangerous thing to do. But adults do not seem to be aware of this. Or perhaps they intentionally turn a blind eye to this unhealthy practice. Youngsters are taken for granted and are expected to be virgins (here, the idea of virginity holds good for both genders) till they get married, which is when they are socially sanctioned to have sex with their spouse.

No one is truly concerned about how a young man or a young woman copes with the fear and insecurity of not knowing anything about sex. While some youngsters deal with their feelings by secretly venturing into the world of sex, a few obedient kids do not learn about it at all. If you think this is good, it is not. In fact,

I would go so far as to say that this is more dangerous than the former. Many marriages are ruined on day one itself because of this complete ignorance, with the partners continuing to live together not just for the sake of society but also because they think that this is how a marriage is supposed to be and that everyone else must be going through the same thing.

In most cases though, youngsters learn about sex from movies and videos, and what they see is what they learn. They don't realize that the actors on the screen are just acting, and are not exactly involved in a mutual sharing and expression of love and sex. They do not know if a particular action actually produces excitement in real life or not. While the videos show people seemingly enjoying the act of sex, they do not show the expressions of love and attachment between two people. So, the youngsters watching these videos conclude, wrongfully so, that sex need not be an expression of love and that it is meant only for carnal pleasure.

The tragedy arises from the fact that there is not even a basic level of sex education in the schools and colleges of our country. Our social and educational systems do not mandate that there be an eligibility criterion that a man or a woman must meet to become a wife or a husband, or, for that matter, even to have sex. Every human being on earth is automatically eligible for the title of husband, wife, mother or father.

How many elders have asked the so-called 'eligible' bachelor if he is indeed eligible for marriage? Eligibility in our society is measured only in terms of the money a man brings into the family. When it comes to a woman, even that is not mandatory.

How many men and women are clear about the additional responsibilities they will have to shoulder when they link another life to their own? Do we ever teach youngsters how to nurture such a newly found relationship? Have any of us advised them to read a good book on sex before getting married? Do we gift couples an educative book on sex so that they become responsible husbands and wives? The answer is a big NO!

When one of the underlying reasons for marriage is safe sex, then why are we so hesitant to talk and learn about it? Why do we not accept that sex requires proper education and learning?

When we talk of 'safe sex', we tend to think only in terms of the physical problems that arise out of unsafe sex. But safe sex also refers to the mental problems that may emerge from not bothering about the likes and dislikes of the partner, and from failing to understand whether the partner is really enjoying the sex and is satisfied with the outcome or not. Only if these things are taken into account will the partner look forward to coming to bed again.

Otherwise, one has to deal with a partner who is unwilling to have sex. Of course, a person can always choose to ignore the facts or not be bothered by them. But how stable will a relationship be under such circumstances?

Think about it: How many women cry after their first experience of sex because of the brutality shown by their sex-starved male partner? How many men get frustrated because there are women who think that sex is an act of barbarism? How many men care to look at the face of the woman they are having sex with to check if she's truly enjoying what he is doing to her or not? How many people are able to make their partners feel loved and respected when they share their bodies with each other?

Sex is all about sharing, but unfortunately, we have learnt that it's only about taking, that if we are enjoying it, there ends the matter! A woman's body can not only bear children, it can also bear a man's attitude—and where she settles for being a passive partner in a sexual relationship, she will not experience the truly liberating pleasures of sex.

7

The Toilet Seat

Intercourse with a woman is sometimes a satisfactory substitute for masturbation.
—Karl Kraus

I WOULD LIKE TO MAKE JUST ONE SMALL CHANGE to the sentence above. I would like to replace 'sometimes' with 'mostly'.

In our society, parents have all the right to beat their children under the pretext of being concerned about their well-being and teaching them a lesson. But the underlying truth is that parents are physically and financially more powerful than their poor children, who are dependent on them and cannot hit them back. Parents take advantage of this simple fact and crush their children's self-esteem. The same thing happens in sex between a man and a woman. A man is physically more powerful than a woman. Nature has bestowed every woman with an open hole in her body into which a man can insert his organ, irrespective of whether she wants it or not. A woman, even if she wishes to, cannot rape a man because a man's organ cannot be forced into her hole unless the man wishes for it. Even if the man is okay with passive sex, unless he gets sexually aroused, a woman cannot force herself upon him.

With children, there is at least a ray of hope that one day, they will grow up and become more powerful than their parents, and can escape from their control. But a woman who is subjected to torture by a man doesn't even have this hope. Isn't it a woman's duty to not say no to her husband any time he wants to have sex? This gives a man an edge over a woman. After getting married and bearing children, many women live as if they cannot pick up the pieces of their lives and walk ahead. But if every woman actually starts doing this, I think at least 50 per cent of marriages would break.

Someone said that sex is a crime because it is always done in secret, in the dark. And since it is done in the dark, one can avoid looking into the eyes of one's partner. This makes it easy to commit this particular crime under the illusion that one's partner is enjoying the act. It is ironical that what is a natural instinct in any living being has become a crime today, simply because of the way we treat it and not because of its original nature.

For many men, a woman is not a partner in bed but is a toilet seat in the washroom. When a man is sexually aroused, he is in a dire state of urgency to get his semen out and he needs a place to eject it into. At that point, he assumes that his wife or female partner or girlfriend is waiting for him to use her like a toilet seat. He can simply go ahead and eject his semen into her hole.

This may seem like too harsh a judgement to pass on men; they do not actually think of women as toilet seats to ejaculate into. But the comparison is unavoidable as most men are under the illusion that ejaculation is what sex is all about. They tend to think that the woman is enjoying the act as much as they are. And of course, there are men who feel that they are superior to women, and that women are simply tools created for their use and pleasure. This is the sort of thought process that leads to rape and forceful sex, both within the institution of marriage and outside of it.

I pity the women, and the men too! They know so little. If they were to sit for an exam on the subject of sex, they would be utter failures. Then again, who taught them about sex? Who assessed them?

Let me now shift gears and talk about the woman who is being used as a toilet seat. The first time a woman has sex with a man, she is mostly going to end up with the impression that this is what sex is all about. She is going to wonder why people give so much importance to it. Out of love and not wanting to hurt the man, she will allow herself to be used as a toilet seat. Fortunately though, this phrase will not cross her mind. But as time passes, the woman will begin to feel utterly bored of the mechanical act of sex. When she crosses the threshold of tolerance, she will feign headaches and tiredness, and use old age and children as reasons to get out of the mundane task.

It would not be fair on my part to continue talking about women and sex if I also do not talk about those women who harass men in bed, either by being indifferent or by refusing to sleep with them for silly reasons. I would say, however, that the real reason for this is that the woman in question does not think of sex as an act of mutual enjoyment. She sees it as a charitable act and behaves as though she is doing the man a favour by agreeing to sleep with him. She may also be angry with the man and want to punish him. All this happens because the woman does not enjoy the act of sex since it does not involve any love. She gets no enjoyment or pleasure out of it. It has also been ingrained into her mind that women don't need sex as much as men do and that this is the way nature has made them.

Believe me, I am not talking about a random, isolated occurrence. In the name of sex and physical relationships, there are dirty things happening in many families. Once, one of my friends told me about the manner in which her husband used to have sex with her. After a tiring day of work, when she would go to sleep; her husband would come and lie down next to her on the bed. He would pull up her saree, insert himself inside her, ejaculate, and then turn around and go to sleep. That was it!

Meanwhile, awakened by his actions, she would just lie on her side with tears in her eyes after he was done, her back facing her husband. When I asked her why she did not stand up for her rights, she said they lived in a single-bedroom house with their two grown-up sons. 'If I refuse to have sex and this guy starts shouting, how will I face my kids?' she asked.

When a man needs to be just a man, he's allowed the right to have extramarital affairs and one-night stands, but a woman is always made to feel guilty if she even thinks beyond engaging in this mundane procedure with someone other than her husband. When she does get an opportunity to sleep with another man and musters her guts to go ahead with it, she always tries to justify her act both to herself and to society.

Sex is as essential as food. While food can be cooked and enjoyed alone, sex needs the involvement of two people. If there is no involvement from both parties, then there can be no enjoyment for them either. Sex is neither a deed of charity nor a weapon of anger. It is a mutual want arising out of love and a desire to be physically close to each other.

I've heard about men who don't touch any part of their partner's body. A man like this just inserts his organ into a woman's vagina, does a few push-ups and comes out energized. I've also heard of men who press a woman's breasts for a few seconds or minutes, then insert themselves into her vagina and ejaculate, as if that is all the woman needs to attain her orgasm. A few 'concerned' men, who claim to know that a woman has to be satisfied before they finish their own 'job', rub her vagina for a few seconds. When they hear her 'aahs' and 'oohs' a few times, they decide that the woman has attained her orgasm. Their duty thus done, they push themselves inside her and ejaculate.

Recently, I was surprised to hear what a man who has been married for fifteen years and has had a few extramarital affairs believes. According to him, when a woman gets wet after arousal is when she orgasms!

The Toilet Seat

After everything is over, when a man asks the woman if she enjoyed herself or not, how would a woman who loves her man have the heart to say no? She might have enjoyed being intimate with him and might have gotten aroused as well, but, at the end of it, she's always left with an incomplete feeling because she never orgasmed. The man gets what he wanted, but she wants more. How long can a woman keep sacrificing her pleasures?

It appears to me that sex is being handled like a mechanical process which has a by-product: A child. But is it enough if a child is born out of sex? Are people having sex merely for the sake of reproduction? How will a person who does not care for his or her partner's happiness and involvement during sex ever enjoy bringing up the by-product of sex? Is this why human beings treat children like they are some lifeless, brainless things? Is this why parents don't allow their children to think on their own or pursue a life of their choice? Is life not about living at all? Strange are the ways of men and women!

Recently, I had a chat with some married women. A few of them were newly married and a few of them had been married for several years. I was thoroughly shocked to hear that they had never been kissed by their husbands—not before sex, not during sex and not after sex. They all said that sex for them was just about allowing their husbands to squeeze their breasts (painfully so), opening their legs wide apart to give the men easy access to their vaginas and then waiting patiently for a few minutes for the whole thing to get over. After the act, their husbands just turned to one side and started snoring, whereas they had to get up, wash themselves and then come back to bed, only to stay wide awake. This is what marriage has done to them; this is what they get for all that they do for the men they are married to.

Some of them told me very innocently, 'I think we need to wait for our next birth to know or enjoy sex, if at all we are to believe your words that it *is* an enjoyable act.'

And that's not the end of all the misconceptions that abound. There are men who believe that the longer they take to ejaculate after inserting themselves into a woman's vagina, the more fun the woman has. When the man does not even do what is required to make a woman attain an orgasm and, for that matter, does not even truly care about her enjoyment, then what is the point in being inside her vagina for a long time? The woman only gets frustrated with the whole thing. In fact, she would be happier if the process ended fast.

It is indeed pathetic that even men who boast of having had many affairs or who proclaim to be 'the best' in bed (I don't know how they came to such a conclusion!), don't have a convincing answer as to how they know if the woman is actually happy in bed or not.

During sex, there's no respect for a woman's feelings, and her likes and dislikes. There's no respect for her body. When questioned about this, the simple answer most men give is, 'Nature has made us like this; you cannot blame us.'

Not only in our society, but across the universe, women seem to suffer men of this type. I am reproducing here an extract from Nancy Friday's book *My Secret Garden: Women's Sexual Fantasies*, which is a compilation of letters and calls she received from women describing their sexual fantasies. This excerpt is from one such account:

> I think you're going to find that all men are really going to get upset about this book of yours. So many of them still think that women are for their enjoyment only. Some won't admit that women (if handled properly) have strong sexual desires and feelings, just as they do. Most men that I ran into before marriage didn't even know what foreplay was. If it becomes more open and publicly known that foreplay is usually necessary to get the ball rolling for the woman,

> I'll bet there'll be a lot more sexually satisfied women than there are now. I had sex with thirty or so men before my husband and never had an orgasm; I always got the ones who jumped on, then jumped off and took me home, and of course I told them they were fantastic lovers and all that, but I felt nothing but frustration.

And then there are men who casually remark that women are simply not interested in sex because they only enjoy taking care of their husbands and kids. These men believe that women derive pleasure from giving, from serving others. Their views about women's needs are based on what they feel they can do for a woman, and not on what the woman actually wants from them in particular and from life in general.

What are women for men like these if not toilet seats?

The Hard Facts

It is unfortunate that even when a man is keen to give his partner the kind of pleasure that he himself derives from sex, he does not know how or what to do. The truth is many women aren't getting the orgasms they want. A few years ago, *Cosmopolitan* published a huge and exhaustive survey, which came up with the following results:

1. Two-thirds of women aged 18–40 said they have faked orgasm.
2. 72 per cent said they'd been with a guy who climaxed, but that the guy didn't even try to return the favour.
3. 38 per cent said they weren't getting enough clitoral stimulation.
4. 50 per cent said, 'I often feel like I'm almost there, but I can't quite get over the edge.'

In the words of Dr David Delvin:

> The most important thing for men to realize these days is that most women want orgasms. A couple of generations ago, many women weren't bothered about not getting an orgasm. Probably many of them didn't even know what an orgasm was. According to doctors, it was 'normal' for a large percentage of women to have no experience of an orgasm. Indeed, as late as the 1970s, there were a few general physicians who maintained that the female orgasm didn't exist and it was simply a myth made up by the media.
> All this has changed now. Today, according to medical opinion, every woman should be able to have orgasms, if she wants to do so.

Results from a research carried out in the UK in 2014 suggest that a majority of women are capable of multiple orgasms, if they wish to have them.

Feigning an Orgasm

Why do many women feign an orgasm?

The first reason could be a lack of awareness about the fact that she too is capable of achieving an orgasm. Believe me, I was once a living example of this. For most of my twenties, I was unaware of what an orgasm was! I used to wonder, after every session of intercourse, what the big deal about sex was. I wondered what people got out of this 'mundane' procedure. I often thought that a woman's body was perhaps just meant for reproduction, while the man's body was made for enjoyment and that this was the reason why men were after sex more than women were.

The second reason is love. The woman loves her partner so much that she doesn't want to hurt his ego by letting him know that he has not been able to make her achieve an orgasm. Ironically, in our society, a man always attaches his manliness to his ability to give pleasure to a woman. So, when he's told that the woman has not achieved an orgasm, it's devastating for him. A woman feigning an orgasm is a woman fanning his ego.

Third, by feigning an orgasm, a woman saves herself from the embarrassment of having to talk about it. Remember, women have been taught not to talk about sex openly, and, even if they want to, there is an inhibition about it.

The fourth reason is that if a man finds out that he's not able to satisfy his partner, he will start wondering if the woman will go and look for another partner. So, feigning an orgasm is a safer option.

Conversely, in some cases, when a man comes to know that his partner is not getting the 'required satisfaction', the woman might fear that the man will go out in search of another partner. The fear of losing him leads the woman to fake an orgasm. She cannot ever tell the man bluntly that he hasn't been satisfying her.

A woman might also feign an orgasm so that the man is done with his act quickly and she can save herself from the torture of having to put up with whatever he was doing.

But isn't it surprising that such feigning goes unnoticed through the years? Is this possible at all? Can a man not know when his partner is faking an orgasm? I think he would certainly know it. But maybe feigning (with the woman feigning orgasm and the man feigning ignorance) has become a mutually convenient habit for both men and women for various reasons.

Alain de Botton, in his book *How to Think More about Sex*, says:

> Erections and lubrication simply cannot be effected by willpower and are therefore particularly true and honest indices of interest. In a world in which fake enthusiasms are rife, in which it is often hard to tell whether people really like us or whether they are being kind to us merely out of a sense of duty, the wet vagina and the stiff penis function as unambiguous agents of sincerity.

Insightful, indeed!

8

Sex as an Expression of Love

THE MAIN REASON WHY PHYSICAL ATTRACTION gets misunderstood as love is because sex is often a manifestation of love. It is the peak expression of love. For example, a woman loves her child from the day it is conceived in her womb. Sometimes, she showers this love on her child delicately, and sometimes with full force of energy in the form of hugs and kisses. The strength and vigour with which love is expressed comes from the intensity with which the love itself flows. Sex is also an outcome of love overflowing from the heart. Sometimes, we just plant a kiss and sometimes we give a hug, and so on. Depending on the dynamics of our relationship, when the intensity of love goes beyond a certain point, it ends in physical intimacy. Thus love transforms itself into a longing to become one with the other person both physically and emotionally, and that brings ecstasy when both people are pulled towards each other the same way. This is why sex is called 'love making' and not 'lust making'.

Once we cross childhood, we lose the physical closeness of the people around us. We miss the reassuring comfort of our parents' hands and their warm touch. We also lose the openness we had as children about our own nudity and start covering most of our bodies. A secrecy sets into our minds. We are taught to behave a certain way, and we are not what we seem to be from the outside.

Alain de Botton says very clearly that the need for sex arises more out of an emotional or psychological need rather than from the arousal of our bodies:

> But deep inside, we never quite forget the needs with which we were born: to be accepted as we are, without regard to our deeds; to be loved through the medium of our body; to be enclosed in another's arms; to occasion delight with the smell of our skin—all of these needs inspiring

our relentless and passionately idealistic quest for someone to kiss and sleep with.

However, we are taught differently. We beg for sex even as we clothe our words with love. The intention is sex, but the medium used is love.

It is a tragedy that we all never learn that sex is an expression of love (some of us do not realize this till the end our lives!).

When a child is born, it becomes one with the universe. It's naturally blessed with a lot of energy, love and warmth to spread around it. We all tend to think that the child needs love from us. But contrary to this belief, the child only needs care and nurturing from us, because it has come into this world as the very personification of love. A human being who is the personification of love need not be taught how to love. However, over the years, as we grow from childhood to adulthood, we start learning and picking up cues from our surroundings. We become corrupted, and we slowly get rid of the love and warmth inside us. This transforms us into creatures that crave love. We reach a point where we need to be taught about love and reminded about how to love. But think about this—a tree need not be taught how to spread its shade; a fish need not be taught how to swim. So why should a man be taught how to love?

Most of us know how temple elephants are tamed. When they are young, one of their legs is chained to a pillar. Every time the elephant tries to move, the chain pulls it back, defeating its attempts to move. By the time the elephant grows up, and becomes big and strong enough to pull off the chain and walk free, it stops making any efforts in this direction because it has become ingrained in its mind by now that it simply *cannot* move. This is what we have done to our children too.

Small children, especially infants, smile at others spontaneously, even if they're not known to them. But do adults smile instantly when they meet strangers? No. This is because unlike an adult, a child is full of love and warmth, and it spreads this love and warmth effortlessly to everyone and everything around it. It is the power of the love within the child that attracts others to it involuntarily.

We all admire the kid who throws a bright smile at us, but when the same bright smile comes from an adult, we label him or her insane. But the insanity actually sets in when we forget to smile at a stranger, when we forget that love is the common thread that keeps the world going.

You might wonder why we're talking about a child here, that too when this is a book on sex. Yes, I do understand that this looks like a digression from the main subject, but actually, it's not. Our childhood, and in particular the way we observe and learn things, decides how we look at sex and love when we become adults. This isn't just a strong connection, it is, in fact, the root of it all.

When a child is born, the new parents boast to the world that they've become mothers and fathers because they're living under the illusion that bringing a child into the world is a huge achievement. They fail to realize that it is a moment to be thankful for, for the child has brought in a fresh wave of energy and happiness into their tiny world. It has turned them into a 'family'. Most importantly, it has brought an abundance of love. But instead of being grateful for all of this, the parents focus on scaling the heights of achievement by grooming their children to be 'good' kids.

Who is a good kid really? A kid who loves its parents and siblings? A kid who respects and listens to its elders? A kid who is obedient, and gets a good name among neighbours and friends? Yes, this is how we define a good kid. But have we ever sat down for a moment and thought about what we are doing?

Who are we to teach a child to love others when it has come into the world as an embodiment of love? Who are we to teach a child to respect others when it is so full of joy, energy, self-respect and self-pride?

Do any of us know why we are teaching all these things to our kids? We lost the love and respect we had for ourselves when we came out of our innocence, all thanks to our parents! And now, we are doing the same thing to our children by letting them use love and respect for others as a combat shield in the field of life. Who wins and who loses here when the child becomes a mere puppet in the world?

Unfortunately, children are treated like puppets by the very people who bring them up by providing them with the basic necessities of life. In exchange for what they give to their children, parents take away a child's self-love and demand respect from them. It is a kind of trade-off, and I would be a hypocrite if I fail to acknowledge that I am as guilty of this as well.

It's not just sex that is a taboo in our society. Even self-love and self-respect are a big no-no. Self-love has been assumed to mean 'selfishness' and self-respect has been equated with 'ego'. These are definitely different things, but how many of us realize this? Self-love and self-respect are the most basic virtues of a human being. Self-love brings self-respect effortlessly along with it. It is a tragedy (in fact, tragedy is an understatement) that we've all been taught to love and respect others while completely washing away all the love and respect we have for ourselves. This is the reason we go around looking for love and respect from others. In fact, we are begging for love and respect, and, in some situations, we also force others to love and respect us.

How can a person whose wealth has been looted completely be charitable to others? There has to be some logic to what we expect, right? When my love and respect for my own self has vanished because I am forced to do things that show how obedient I am, how can I express genuine love for someone else? Every soul is as free as the air around it. But when we try to squeeze it into a particular shape or pattern, the soul loses itself. This is precisely the reason why some people go in search of the self at a later stage in life after discovering the futility of living. But how can we search for ourselves in such a large universe? How can we find something we lost ages ago when we were innocent children?

Only a loveless heart becomes a self-centred heart. We know that we don't have love and respect for ourselves in our hearts. So, we assume that the other person too doesn't have love and respect in their heart. Even though this is an illusion created by the lack of self-love and self-respect, there arises in us the need to safeguard our interests. Consequently, we become self-centred and egoistic.

As parents, teachers and elders, we need to live a life of love and respect. Children observe us and our actions very closely, and they intuitively learn from what they see. Love and respect need not be taught to them in so many words. In fact, love and respect can never really be taught. If children see their parents loving and respecting each other, they, in turn, will love every man and woman they come across. We know that actions speak louder than words, but I would say that actions alone are enough; the rest will fall into place automatically.

If someone is brought up in an environment where love and respect are part of the natural behavioural pattern of people, they will see sex as an expression of love. And when they are deeply in love with someone, their feelings will naturally culminate in physical intimacy. But if the other person doesn't want to get physical with them or doesn't reciprocate their feelings, the heart, which is full of love and respect for itself, will not demean itself by forcing its desires upon the unwilling other. Such a heart can only make love, it cannot demand sex, because true love transcends sex.

The heart that is in love looks at life as a beautiful and enjoyable experience, and it sees sex as a natural flow of energy. This heart knows that sex is not a sin but is as beautiful as love itself. So, when two people are full of love for each other and give each other pleasure that is beyond description, the act of sex becomes a virtue; for them, and between them, it can never be a sin.

9

Extramarital Affairs

WHEN SEX ITSELF IS NOT SEEN IN THE RIGHT perspective, then how can extramarital affairs ever be tolerated?

But let us look at first things first. Human beings are not monogamous by nature, and the restrictions on sex between a man and a woman were brought in to instil a degree of discipline in our social lives.

Given that human beings are not monogamous, there is no reason to wonder why people have extramarital affairs. However, we don't have the understanding or the empathy to comprehend why a person does so.

We've been conditioned to think that a person can be in love and have sex with only one person. If this number goes beyond one, then the person is treated like a criminal.

Most of us look at things as being just black or white; we turn a blind eye to the possibility of there being grey areas in between. We may try to live in denial, but the truth is that extramarital affairs have existed ever since the institution of marriage came into force. What was once the privilege of men alone has now spread its wings and caught up with the women too.

But why do people have extramarital affairs? It could be a variety of factors that lead them to this decision: A loveless marriage, an unsatisfactory sexual relationship, a tendency to explore, a genuine love or attraction springing between two people who are not married to each other, or monotony.

Let us deal with these scenarios case by case.

A Loveless Marriage

Marriage is an oath taken by two people to love each other till the end of their lives. This, in itself, is an irony since no one can be forced to love another person! Love takes its own sweet time to develop and follows its own course. Keeping two people tied in a knot without love in their hearts will only lead to a vegetative existence for both. One of them might try to pull at the knot too hard and may fume within when it doesn't come undone. This can give rise to hatred or indifference in the marriage. In some cases, a loveless relationship exists due to tolerance and compromise, qualities we boast of without realizing that their presence in excess can make our lives miserable.

Philosophically speaking, if you're in love, you must not expect anything in return. However, we've all learned a different kind of love, one that is rooted in our needs, and whoever fills these needs unconsciously, becomes an object of our love. This need for love can assume any shape or form; it can be both tangible and intangible. For instance, we may feel light and happy after spending time with a particular person. We may like something in the other person. Or the other person may make us feel good about ourselves. This leads us to think that we love that person because we experience a certain kind of happiness or completeness when we're with this person. It is this feeling that we describe as 'love'.

Naturally, when this other person is unable to continue giving us the same happiness or satisfaction, the person slowly or suddenly ceases to be the object of our love.

Also, love is expressed more through touch than through the words we speak. When this need is not taken care of properly, there is every chance that the love may start diminishing.

How many people realize that when there is a deep union of two minds, even a tight hug or a quick, fleeting kiss can be sexually more satisfying than intercourse itself? If two minds are not in union, nothing they do with their bodies can give them any pleasure.

If you can't make your marriage work, get out of it. Live your life and let the other person also live their life. Don't use your children as an excuse to stay in the marriage. Don't say that the children need both parents to grow up well. You are only setting a bad example of what a marriage and a family should be like. While living with parents who are in harmony is the best thing that can happen for children, it's better for them to live with one caring parent rather than two parents who are teaching them hypocrisy as a way of life.

An Unsatisfactory Sexual Relationship

Let us accept the fact that the basis for marriage is companionship, and that this includes sharing the pleasures of the body as well. While I strongly believe that love should lead to sex, I also believe, just as strongly, that when the sex between two people is not mutually satisfactory, indifference can set in slowly, in spite of them being in love with each other. This is because sex is one of the basic necessities of life, and physical intimacy helps to create and retain emotional intimacy to a large extent.

A man or a woman can be loving, understanding and genuinely nice, but what if either of them turns out to be a disaster in bed? Or if they refuse to have sex with their partner? Clearly, there is something wrong here.

But how many of us sit down with our partners, and candidly discuss what we like and don't like while having sex? A woman may, for example, not like to do something in bed, but she might continue doing it just to please her husband because that's what he wants and enjoys. The husband, on the other hand, might not even be aware that his wife is doing it just to keep him sexually happy, even though she herself hates it.

Women are also told not to exhibit a craving for sex. Most women pretend to be passive partners because that's what they've been conditioned to be. Even when a man expects her to participate more actively in the act, the woman's well-trained brain may refuse to do so. After a while, the man will naturally lose interest in her because of the lack of active participation from her. An open, heart-to-heart discussion on this matter could help. However, in most cases, the man and the woman will not do so.

A major reason many women find themselves in an unsatisfactory sexual relationship is the fact that they start getting fully aroused only when the man ejaculates. By this time, however, the man has spent all his force and energy. For him, the sex is over. So, he withdraws and, in most cases, promptly goes off to sleep while the poor woman is left wanting. Had they not been having sex, the woman would've probably enjoyed peaceful sleep at least. But now, just as she is ready to satisfy her sexual craving, the man literally leaves her in the lurch, without even a warm hug! Think of the woman's plight in this situation. Think of how loathsome it would be for her.

Being a woman, I was shocked to learn that the reverse also happens. I was talking about this book to one of my male friends when he confided to me in private that his wife doesn't give in to any of his sexual advances. She mostly acts as though sex is a detestable thing and makes him feel bad about wanting to have sex. However, every once in a while, she makes sexual advances herself and gets him to do things for her. And once she achieves an orgasm, she just gets up and walks out of bed.

All along, I had been under the assumption that such things happened only to women and that men always got their way. My friend's revelation was an eye-opener. When I shared his story with another man, he too confided that he'd been living like this for many years. He said that every time his wife came near him, he nursed the hope that his physical needs would be taken care of. But it always ended badly.

One of these two men is no longer in the marriage. The other man has children, and so he continues to be with his wife. He says he has no other choice but to discreetly look for other women to appease his physical needs.

Though solutions and remedies to such problems can be reached within the marriage, they are normally sought outside. This is, of course, because of the taboo attached to sex that keeps couples from discussing their issues.

I once had a conversation with a man who had been married for more than five years. He said, 'Every time I ask my wife whether what I'm doing is to her liking or not and if she would like me to do something else that would make her happy, she says there's nothing that she looks for and that she's enjoying my actions. Sometimes, I feel she is happy. But mostly, I get the feeling that she's just tolerating me. In the end, she says she enjoyed the sex. But even after all these years together, I'm not sure about what she likes and dislikes. If she really enjoys what I'm doing, then why does she say no to my advances most of the times?'

'Make her talk,' I told him. 'Make her understand that her enjoyment matters to you; that you cannot enjoy sex completely with all these doubts running around in your mind.'

This conversation made me understand that even if a husband is genuinely concerned about his wife's enjoyment, she might not want to talk about it openly. And while the man realizes that this could create a rift between them, the woman doesn't seem to think so because such is her upbringing.

Tendency of the Man or Woman to Explore

People are different. People are unique. Some may be obedient in mind and action, while some may be obedient in action alone. And then there are people who wish to live their one life completely, by following what their mind wants with their actions.

There are people who live in their place of birth forever and there are those who move to a different city for work. There are adventurous people who like to visit new places, have new experiences, live in different weather conditions, meet people from different cultures and sample different cuisines.

Similarly, there are people who like to explore different kinds of relationships too. There are men and women who want to experience different kinds of sexual joys with different people. They could be married or single, but their relationship status does not define them. Their actions do.

Whoever said that a married man cannot get attracted to a woman other than his wife or that a married woman cannot find attraction outside her marriage? It is our social conditioning that has made us think so. We cannot find fault with people who follow their hearts in search of love. At least, they are not being hypocrites. Are you shocked by this? Surprised?

Well, you shouldn't be. We're not just mindless, heartless children-producing machines. We are naturally prone to get attracted to people belonging to the opposite sex or the same sex, though not to everyone. People whom we perceive as good-looking or good-hearted, and with whom we vibe well as they have the same mental frequency as us are bound to attract us.

Attraction towards another person creates an emotion in our hearts. I strongly believe that 99 per cent of people experience this attraction and emotion towards at least one person other than their spouse or partner in their lifetime.

There are people who think this isn't right as they have a partner and they shouldn't cheat on them. So, they try to banish such emotions from their hearts. There are others who live with the emotion, but don't act upon it, again for the same reason cited earlier or because they are afraid of being caught, afraid of rejection and afraid of losing what they already have in their life.

On the other side are people who want to experiment in life. They might want to explore sex and may find it easier to do so with a person whom they will never meet again in life because the fear of being looked down upon as a weird person is absent in this case. They might plunge into such an exploration and take calculated risks. Some are smart enough to get into a new relationship without encountering any problems. However, this is not for everyone. Depending on the circumstances, we have to understand if the person is worth taking a risk for. Just like in business plans, we should always assess the risks involved. We should go ahead and act on our emotions only if we're bold enough to face the worst.

I'm not advocating that everyone should explore love outside marriage. I'm only saying that there are different perspectives in life, different ways of looking at things. Just because a person is adventurous, they cannot be termed a 'bad' person. As long as they fulfil their responsibilities towards their families and dependents at home, and continue to genuinely take care of their needs and keep their people happy without sacrificing their own happiness, I don't see what the problem is.

A Genuine Love Springing Between Two People Who Are Not Married to Each Other

A loving heart will keep falling in love throughout its life. The idea of there being only one love doesn't exist for such a heart. But haven't you heard many dialogues to the contrary in the movies? In almost every romantic film, the hero says to his lady love, 'I've just one heart and only you can occupy it. There is no place for anyone else in it.'

How can this be possible? Love keeps happening. Love keeps blooming. A person can love as many people as their heart can hold. They can fall in love as many times as the opportunities arise, with as many people as they come across.

Our ancestors devised monogamy in marriage as a way to discipline us. Marriage is an institution that has its own values. It provides people with a lot of convenience. You create a family, you take care of your people and they take care of you in turn. The man gives his wife what she wants and she gives him what he wants. Your parents give you what you want when you're growing up and you give them what they want when they are ageing. This is all a system of creating conveniences. And love is not always the basis of marriage. Convenience is the primary basis of marriage.

Love, in truth, is spontaneous. Its nature is not to get bound by legal bondages. Laws or social norms cannot force someone to love another person. Norms can only enforce certain physical or financial duties and obligations.

When we get married, we take up the responsibility of caring for our spouse and family. We respect our family and support them, financially and physically. But love happens on its own. It may or may not happen in a marriage. Even if it happens, there is every chance that either partner may meet someone they like and fall in love with them.

I had a colleague in one of the companies I worked for and on the few occasions that I met his wife, I saw her love for her husband in her eyes. That is something rare to see. Rarer still because this colleague and his wife weren't newly-weds; they had, in fact, been married for almost twenty years. I could still see the love glowing in their eyes whenever they looked at each other. It was as though their courting period had never ended!

One day, I had the opportunity to talk to my colleague alone. I told him how incredible it was to see the love between him and his wife, and how I was really happy for him. I am an open person and people generally talk to me about their personal matters without any inhibition. When he told me proudly that he was the reason for her everlasting love for him, I responded with a typical, 'Yeah, of course! It also has to depend on you, naturally.'

The Toilet Seat

However, I was absolutely surprised by what he said next: 'She has an affair with one of her distant relatives who lives in the West. Once in a while, she visits him and spends time with him, and I take care of the kids when she is away.'

'Wow!' I exclaimed. 'Then I should look up to you more than I look up to her. But tell me, men normally don't accept all this. How are you so cool about it?'

His response is what I really want to share here: 'Look, she loves me and she has always loved me. She takes great care of me, my kids and my mom who is old. She has all that a man can look for in a woman. But I know she also loves him a lot. In spite of this love, her love for me hasn't diminished in any way. Meeting him every once in a while and spending time with him gives her happiness. This happiness spreads automatically when she's at home. Because I don't talk about it and embarrass or shame her, she loves me more every day. You may say that guilt makes her love me more and take better care of me, but guilt cannot result in love.

'And you say that you see her love for me in her eyes. Isn't that sufficient for me to lead a happy life with her? We have two kids, and we shower a lot of love on them. Her responsibilities towards me as a wife are more than the responsibilities she has for this other person, because we have created a family together and we support each other to keep our family intact. But love need not be and cannot be measured. That is the way I look at it. She has the freedom to do what she wants, and she has the heart to love me as well as him. I don't see anything wrong in this.'

'But doesn't this make you think that you can also be with anyone you want? Will she be okay if you do the same thing?' I asked him.

'First of all, I don't have anyone so close to me, like she has him. But there is no need for me to scout for someone just because she has someone else. Then love is not what I've understood it to be. Second, we have a great time whenever we're together. We don't discuss this other part of her life because it doesn't have anything to do with what I am doing. Perhaps one day, I too may fall in love with someone. But I'm not sure that will happen. And even if it happens, I don't know whether I'll tell her about it or not. Nothing else matters as long as we're happy together and in our individual lives. Everything is all right as long as we're responsible towards each other and towards the rest of our family.'

I learned a lot from this discussion. It gave me a clearer understanding of love. If everyone could think like him, the world would be a much better place to live in. Imagine how beautiful life would be for people with a clear understanding and a loving heart.

But what do we hear day in and day out? What do we read in the newspapers? That a husband strangled his cheating wife. That a wife burned her husband's lover. Where is love here? Where is the understanding and the sense of responsibility? There is only sex, only the partner's body that seems to bother everyone, which gets all the importance. Everyone wants the body to be pure and untouched by anyone else.

Who cares if the woman is a pain in the neck or the man is a drunkard, and beats up his wife and children every day? As long as one does not have sex with another person, he is the perfect person. He is Ram's avatar. However, even Ram had questioned his wife's chastity.

Monotony

Just think of this situation: In the beginning of a marriage or courtship, everything about the other person intrigues us. We want to know more about the person, we want to see more of them. We are curious about the way they speak, think, dress and undress. Everything is new to us. So, every minute that we spend with the other person is interesting and enjoyable.

Consciously or unconsciously, we make a lot of effort to impress the other person with an outward show of affection and appreciation. But all of this diminishes in the course of time.

Within a few years, we become so used to each other that nothing is new to us anymore. We know how the other person will respond in any situation. We've seen and felt each's other body. Every part of it. The same touch and the same reactions feel boring. Unconsciously, we start losing interest in the other person as the excitement quotient vanishes gradually. Even among couples who have loving, healthy and enjoyable sex, there is a big chance of monotony setting in.

The arrival of children too adds to this lack of interest. As parents, we have more responsibilities to shoulder. There is more and more work to do, both inside and outside the house. And as the children grow older, our concern for their lives also starts growing.

We need a lot of enthusiasm, light-heartedness and a certain kind of wild indiscipline to have enjoyable sex. But because we are shuttling between our various duties and responsibilities almost all the time, sportive sex becomes an unachievable goal.

Naturally then, when we meet someone new and find something in them that fits our interests, we tend to get attracted to them.

Summing Up

Whoever finds pleasure outside their marriage should always remember to manage things at home properly.

After all, their family is their responsibility. One has no right to hurt their family or deprive them of their time and love. The basic rule should be this: I need my happiness, and I'm able to find it outside my marriage, but my people at home also need their happiness, so, I must keep them happy by balancing everything.

Taking up the responsibility of a family is our choice. The way we live is our own choice. The work we do is also our choice. But at times, everything seems to be a burden and our happiness, which is the ultimate goal of our life, is not attained. We then start seeing our loved ones as unnecessary baggage. When we start thinking like this, can we ever give them any happiness and care? When we don't find happiness and love in ourselves, is it possible for us to give love to the people around us? We are neither happy ourselves nor do we spread happiness around us.

But money and work are not the only things in life that make one happy or unhappy. There are several other things, both small and big, that determine one's happiness. Love is one such important factor and time is another.

We are all conditioned to think that love happens only once and with one person, especially when it concerns falling in love with a person of the opposite sex. What I don't understand here is this: Love is just love, so how can there be varieties of love? Just because we tend to get physically intimate with the opposite sex, do we believe that this kind of love is different from love in general? If change is the only constant in life, why can't we accept the fact that a person with a loving heart can keep falling in love with many people, over and over again?

What if a person finds some attractive quality in a person who is not one's spouse? What if the other person also finds something attractive in him/her? This is quite natural and it happens to almost everyone. Only a few of us, however, will live naturally, going beyond social conditioning. To understand and accept this, one has to understand the concept of marriage and family in a more practical sense.

10

Going Beyond Trust

I'VE SEEN PEOPLE WHO DOUBT THEIR SPOUSES and I've also heard people say, 'I trust him/her completely.' While the former way of thinking appears 'bad' and the latter sound 'good', I would say nothing is ideal in life. In a relationship, people should go beyond trust—and I really mean this.

When someone has doubts about his or her partner's fidelity, the love in the relationship simply ends. But when they say they trust their partner and believe that they will not do something to break that trust, they actually reveal an underlying distrust. What they are saying is that their partner may break their trust, that there are chances that he or she will do it, but they will choose not to do it. Essentially, there is some kind of an analysis going on inside their mind. Let us suppose that one fine day, someone reliable tells them that they saw their spouse or partner doing something unworthy of their trust. Unconsciously, they will start analysing if he could've really done this. Then they will come to the conclusion that, given the circumstances, either he could've or could not have done something to breach their trust. This is not a good basis for a relationship. Calculations like this will weaken the relationship over a period of time.

To sustain a relationship, one has to go beyond trust. When a husband tells his wife that he will be late in coming back home from work since he has a meeting to attend, the matter ends right there. The wife must accept this at face value. But let us assume that someone is sitting next to the woman when the man calls to tell her that he is going to be late. Once the woman ends the call, this person asks her if her husband indeed has work in office or does she think he is going out with someone else?

A suspicious wife is likely to say, 'Who knows? He is capable of it.' In this case, it's evident that the wife has always looked at her husband with suspicion. Where does her love for him go in such a situation?

But if the woman is trusting, she'll probably say, 'Not at all, he's not that kind of a person. I know him.' Here, the wife thinks that her husband wouldn't do anything to hurt her; she has faith in him. Underneath this faith, however, there is always an iota of distrust because we all know that a person can change any time. A trustworthy person can become untrustworthy when presented with the right circumstances and opportunities. The second situation is actually more dangerous than the first. In the first situation, the wife can handle the truth when it comes out, but in the second situation, the woman will suffer a heartbreak and an absolute loss of trust.

What would be truly ideal would be the woman going beyond trust and saying, 'Why should I even think about these things? He has told me that he will be late and that is all that I need to know because I had to decide whether I should cook for him or not, and if I should wait for him before I go out.' And there ends the matter. She doesn't analyse anything. She doesn't waste her time and energy on needless thoughts. She's a woman who loves her man completely. People may say this is indifference. But it's definitely not that. Only if the woman is not bothered about her partner's safety or health can you call it indifference. Here, she has been assured that her husband is safe and that he will be eating his dinner in office. There is nothing for her to worry about. She does not need to know anything else. This is love. This can only be love.

Going beyond trust is not about being bothered about when someone is worthy of that trust or not. It's about accepting the other person, giving them the space they require as individuals, and not getting into unnecessary assumptions and judgments, not poking our nose and wasting our precious time and energy wondering about things that may not even exist or happen. Going beyond trust is about spending beautiful times together, and also making our own time more peaceful and productive.

11

Friendship as the Basis of a Relationship

I RECENTLY READ A QUOTE BY ELLA WHEELER Wilcox which says, 'All love that has not friendship for its base, is like a mansion built upon the sand.'

There's another interesting quote about friendship which my friend had shared with me quite a long time ago: 'Friendship is like a mansion and it has room for everything.'

While the first quote proves the point that friendship is above any relationship, the second beautifully highlights the point that friendship gives space for people to be who they are as individuals, despite the closeness of their bond.

The most beautiful thing about friendship is that we don't try to possess our friends. We respect them as individuals and don't treat them like our possession. But this is not how things are in a romantic or matrimonial relationship.

My friend has many friends, some known and some unknown to me, but I'm not bothered about this. Whenever I think of him or I see him, I know that we are friends who love each other. His having ten or hundred other friends doesn't make me think that he's no longer my friend or that his love for me has diminished. I don't wonder, even for a second, if he has lost interest in me, or if there is something lacking in either me or our friendship.

When such thoughts don't arise in a friendship, why do they emerge in romantic and matrimonial relationships, even though we proclaim that the relationship is based on love and friendship?

Friendship is a natural feeling that doesn't care for rules and regulations. Also, there are no demands in friendship. When I call a friend and ask him if he's free to watch a movie with me and he says no, citing some reason or the other, I don't sit and analyse the reason. I simply say, 'That's okay, probably some other day. Let me know when you're free, we'll go for a movie then.'

When you tell a friend that you don't have the time to see him, he says, 'Fine. We'll meet some other time.' A friend says, 'Oh, you want to see me today? Tell me when and where you want to meet.' Or, 'Oh, you're out of town and your father isn't well? Don't worry, I'll take him to the doctor and take care of him. And don't worry about the money; we'll sort it out when you are back.' A friend also says, 'I don't agree with what you're doing, but I'll still stand by you.'

There are no feelings of being betrayed or ignored. There is no guilt. Period. But all hell breaks loose if the same thing happens between a husband and a wife. Why?

Perhaps it is so because we don't exercise control over a friend. A friend is a friend and nothing else. You can talk about anything with a friend and get away with it. A friend can give you a suggestion, but they don't expect you to adhere to it. A friend argues with you, but doesn't fight. He doesn't say, 'I'm good to you, I support you, so you have to abide by my rules and regulations.' He doesn't assume authority over you.

For instance, let's say that my friend introduces me to one of his new friends and, for some reason, I don't end up liking this new friend. I can tell my friend that I don't like his new friend and that he should not expect me to hang out with the two of them. I will never say, 'I don't like your new friend, so you must end your friendship with him.'

But think of the same scenario unfolding between a man and a woman who are in a romantic relationship. Either the new relationship has to end or the old one will vanish!

It's important to nurture friendship in every relationship, not just in the relationship between a husband and a wife. Imagine, if there is friendship between parents and their children, and among siblings and in-laws, wouldn't our lives be simpler?

Friendship doesn't imprison you; instead, it frees you. It doesn't force anything on you. It doesn't even insist that you always be a friend or that you cannot have other friends.

Whatever be the relationship—parent-child, teacher-student, husband-wife, or the bond between siblings—let the foundation be friendship. If you really love someone, allow them some space when they want it, cuddle them when they want you near them. You don't have to always stand with them. You have to stand by them like a true friend. That is more important than anything else.

If you allow friendship to be the basis for every relationship, you'll see what wonders it does to your relationships.

12

Desperation

WHY IS THERE A SENSE OF DESPERATION among people when it comes to sex? Why do people keep pressurizing others to have sex with them when the other person is not interested? Of course, there is nothing wrong in being attracted to someone. But when your advances are rejected, should you not leave it at that and perhaps just continue with a friendship?

Maybe the difficulty to do so is because sex always seems to dominate the minds of people and this makes them desperate to have sex at any point in time. Some people try to camouflage their desperation for sex with proclamations of love. But the moment they realize that you are not willing to have sex with them, you can rest assured that their 'love' for you will vanish that very instant.

Desperation causes all kinds of perversions, which, in turn, lead to all kinds of horrible things happening in society. From the molestation and rape of newborn babies and old women to the sexual exploitation of children by their own parents, desperation makes a person lose all their dignity and humanity in the pursuit of appeasing their hunger.

Wet chats, sexting with strangers, not knowing anything about them and sometimes not even knowing their gender or age are all outcomes of sexual deprivation and the resultant desperation.

But why are people so desperate for sex? What makes them behave in such a disgusting manner?

The universe is filled with men and women of all kinds. Both genders exist to complement each other. Men and women live together at home, work together at the workplace and interact with each other in different capacities all the time. But in the name of discipline and protection, society often tries to keep boys and girls away from each other. Why are there separate schools and colleges for girls and boys? Why are there separate queues for men and women wherever they go? Why are we, as a society, creating so many barriers between men and women? It's these very barriers and restrictions that make boys and girls curious about each other. And this curiosity to find out more about the opposite sex makes them indulge in stealthy acts. But if society allows them to live naturally and mingle with each other, such things will not happen. Friendships will blossom between men and women, and they will start respecting each other's space. The more the secrecy and distance that is created between them, the more curious and desperate they become to know what is hidden and forbidden.

About 99 per cent of parents don't allow their children free access to sex education. Neither do they talk to their children about sex nor do they explain everything to them. Remember, today's youngsters are tomorrow's elders. And when youngsters don't understand the basics of sex, when they don't know what could create a strong foundation for a good relationship, they falter. They experience deprivation and become desperate, and this doesn't bode well for the future of our society.

Most of us don't feel complete when it comes to sex. There is always a craving for more because very rarely, if ever, do we experience fulfilment in our sexual relationships. This is because we don't understand sex completely. As I quoted right at the beginning of this book, we think about sex a lot, but we think about it in the wrong way.

So, even though we might be aware that there is something wrong in the foundation we have laid for raising our children, we keep complaining about people being desperate or perverted. When the root is completely damaged, what's the point in spraying medicine over the leaves of the tree?

13

Masturbation

It's easy, fun and no one gets hurt.
—Louis C.K.
*I'm a promoter of masturbation. Don't sleep around ...
learn yourself first!
Guys do it, but girls don't. They should.*
—Taylor Momsen

EVERY PERSON HAS TO TAKE SOME TIME OUT TO be alone. That is when they learn more about themselves and that is when their creativity blossoms. This is 100 per cent true. A person who loves to be with his or her own self, who takes time out to travel within their own self is one who can love others and respect them as distinct individuals.

Many great thinkers have said that solitude is not a void. Solitude is not loneliness; it's just being alone with oneself—and being alone is not a negative thing. In my opinion, nothing can be more positive and uplifting than the ability to be alone.

I would say the same thing for masturbation as well, although in a different sense. Everyone should learn to attain an orgasm with oneself, at least every now and then.

There is nothing wrong with masturbation. In fact, it's the right thing to do. It's good for us to be with our own self sometimes, to explore our bodies ourselves and enjoy an orgasm with the self. This solves a lot of problems and does a lot of good for the general health of sexual relationships.

When a teenage boy or girl learns to masturbate and achieve an orgasm, they don't get too desperate to explore sexual activities with another person when they're not yet old and responsible enough to handle the consequences of their actions. The pent-up sexual energy within their bodies finds release without the need for another person's help. When youngsters learn masturbation the proper way, they learn to be self-reliant during times of need. They also learn that there is no need to pursue the opposite sex desperately.

They learn to wait for the right time, when they feel fit enough to take care of the outcomes of their actions.

Myth: Masturbation Is Injurious to Health

Sexologists and relationship counsellors frequently encounter patients who hold the belief that masturbation is injurious to health. In a Rediff article titled '"Is masturbation harmful?" Misconceptions about sex', author Matthew Schneeberger quotes Dr Prakash Nanalal Kothari, a Mumbai-based sexologist, who says, 'Some patients believe that excessive masturbation leads to impotence, tuberculosis and homosexuality.' This, however, is completely untrue. In the same article, Dr Kothari goes on to explain:

> Masturbation is as normal as sexual intercourse ... What happens to the penis when it is inside the vagina during sexual intercourse is the same as what happens when it is inside the folded palm during masturbation ... There is nothing like excessive masturbation, which results in the weakening of the genitals. The tongue does not grow weak in one who is talkative. Neither does it become strong if one observes silence![1]

---

1 Matthew Schneeberger, '"Is masturbation harmful?" Misconceptions about sex', *Rediff*, https://www.rediff.com/getahead/2008/aug/04sex.htm, accessed on 24 January 2025.

To reiterate his argument, Dr Kothari drew an interesting parallel between the act of masturbation and proficiency in English, saying, 'If you have a good grounding in English, it will be easier to pick up friends. Similarly, if you have experience with masturbation, it will be easier when the time comes for intercourse.'

Unfortunately, masturbation is generally something that people resort to out of desperation when they don't have a partner to satisfy them. But in such a situation, masturbation creates a lonely feeling, and sometimes even a sense of shame sets in. What people forget is that whatever is made possible by nature cannot be a thing of shame. As George Carlin says, 'If God intended us not to masturbate, he would've made our arms shorter.' If you still have doubts, you can check with a sexologist.

> *'Don't knock masturbation. It's sex with someone I love.'*
>
> —Woody Allen

Just like solitude gives you time for introspection, masturbation gives you time to explore your body. It lets you know which part of your body is ticklish and which part, when touched, rubbed or squeezed, brings you ecstasy. This knowledge will help you in leading your partner to the right places and action when you are with him or her, and that, in turn, will give you a high.

When people believe that everything is possible within them and understand that there is nothing wrong or shameful about doing things with one's own self, masturbation then is a natural way of appeasing one's sexual appetite, leading to fewer perversions in society. I'm not saying that masturbation will completely get rid of all perversions, but I'm sure a change in people's mindset about masturbation will definitely bring down their sexual desperation and the resultant perversions.

When you know and love your body well, sex with the opposite gender becomes more pleasurable. It will happen out of love and not desperation. There will then be a natural feeling of togetherness and a sharing of love. Sex will be more than just a physical act of relieving oneself.

When you learn to enjoy solitude, you'll look for people you can share your time with, people who will enrich your life. You won't be desperate to be with someone just because you're lonely. You'll know that your solitude is worth more than you wasting your time with unwanted people. When you learn to be alone with your body, you learn to love yourself. You will not be desperate to get into bed with anyone and everyone you meet. You'll choose to share your body and your self with the person you love. And you'll be in a position to appreciate the warmth the other person brings to your side. You will relish the love that is showered on you and you will cherish the moments you spend with this person.

I can always cook and then eat what I cook. But when I cook for someone else and see them enjoy my food, that gives me much more pleasure. Only love can achieve this. And this is possible only when I love myself.

Proper education on sex, including masturbation, will lead to the development of a healthy outlook on sex and love. The more self-reliant people are, the more careful they will be in selecting their partners because they will know that in the absence of a partner, they can still enjoy their solitude and that they need not get desperate to be in a relationship. When there is no desperation, your heart and brain work better, and are in sync with each other.

Among all types of sexual activity, masturbation is, however, the one in which the female most frequently reaches orgasm

> — Alfred Charles Kinsey in his book
> *Sexual Behavior in the Human Female*

14

The Institution Called Marriage

AS A YOUNGSTER, I WAS MADE TO BELIEVE THAT marriage was a necessary social institution that brought discipline into the lives of people, and that family was the basis of a support system that helped one live a life without hassles. However, when I grew older and got married myself, I saw that there was a lot of ugliness within the institution of marriage. Every interaction with other married people further confirmed this belief. I couldn't see any connection between the men and women who were married to each other. Now, I know that marriage can connect people only legally and physically. There is, alas, no connection between their hearts, for that can happen only if there is love and respect between them.

Recently, I read an article which said that in India, 90 per cent of marriages are still arranged and that the divorce rate is just 1 per cent.[2] But should we really be boasting about this statistic? Does it really reflect the reality of the situation? Is it only the number of legal divorces that should be counted to determine the divorce rate in arranged marriages? There are many people living separately without being legally divorced. What about them? They may have valid reasons for doing so—they may feel that there is no need for a legal divorce as long as they are leading a peaceful life or they might not want to go through the pains of battling a divorce in court.

There are also people who live together under the same roof without there being any connections or bonding between them. They may be doing so because of their children, because of financial reasons or some convenience the arrangement brings to them or because of social conditioning. To the world outside, they are a legal couple. But are they a *loving* couple?

---

2   'Love Marriages Vs. Arranged Marriages in India'- www.ichhori.com/2021/11/love-marriages-vs-arranged-marriages

If the fate of arranged marriages is this, then so-called 'love' marriages are a disaster as well. In arranged marriages, people do not tend to assume mutual compatibility right from the beginning. They know beforehand that they will have to compromise a lot and put in massive efforts to understand each other. But people who marry for 'love' are mostly under the illusion that they've already understood each other well since they are 'made for each other'. They don't realize that while everything is hunky-dory during the courtship period, it's only when people start living together that they actually come to see the various facets of one another's personality, especially the sides that they don't like. When marital responsibilities have to be shouldered, people understand just how much they are willing to take up, if at all. Over time, these responsibilities either become a burden that they want to shirk or they fulfil these duties to perfection.

There is also a very strong tendency to take ownership of the person they have married. People expect their spouse to behave the way they want them to. Is this a practical expectation to have? And how many people have their own expectations met? It's also obvious that when expectations are not met, frustration sets in, leading to petty fights and differences cropping up. In love marriages too things get ugly. Like those in arranged marriages, people also tend to continue being in these troubling love marriages for various reasons. They don't want to get out. One of the reasons could be ego—they don't want to show others that they have failed in sustaining their marriage, especially since they got into it willingly. This is also the reason some of them believe that they have to stay in the marriage until the very end. Some people may be scared of their family's reaction, especially their parents who may take the 'we-told-you-so' stance. Yet others don't have the support of their family; they don't have anyone to turn to for help or counselling.

Marriages can be called 'successful' only if, after many years of marriage, the couple still loves each other's company, still continues to have mutually enjoyable sex, and if they love and care for each other in the same way as they did during their early years. Couples who are in a successful marriage must be able to say, with full conviction, that their marriage 'rocks' when someone asks them how their married life is.

But there are people who might say, 'What is the point in cribbing about one's partner? Even if I had married someone else, life would've been the same. I would've probably had the same problems with my marriage.' Why do they say this? Is it to prove that marriage is a necessary evil? And if it's a necessary evil that is going to cost us our freedom, peace and happiness, why embrace it so fiercely? Is marriage meant only to ensure that people have sanctioned sex and procreate? Is that all there is to it?

On the brighter side, we can look at how marriages provide us with companionship for a lifetime. When we're married, we have someone to turn to in times of need. Marriage is a convenience. We take up different responsibilities, and complement each other in bringing happiness and peace into each other's life. Marriage enables you to savour the joys of parenting together. But if there is no companionship in a marriage, what is the point of being in it?

Let us deal with arranged marriages—the most advocated and favoured system in Indian society.

Here, a single person can live life on their own only till a certain age, beyond which they're expected to get married to fulfil their need for sex.

Marriage, in other words, facilitates sex. Of course, along with sex, there are other comforts too—the comfort of a home, of having someone to cook for you and take care of your needs. So, ultimately, people get into a trade-off in the name of marriage; a kind of barter where they tell each other, 'I'll give you these things and you give me these things.' Sometimes, the terms and conditions are discussed beforehand, and sometimes they are left unspoken and are taken for granted.

Let us look into the following scenarios:

1. Love happens at first sight, blossoms and grows as the days go by, and the couple lives happily ever after. (The probability of this is very low.)
2. Love emerges over a period of time and, thereafter, grows stronger every day. (Again, the probability of this is low, though it is slightly more than scenario 1.)
3. Love happens either at first sight or after some time, but it vanishes after a point of time. But the couple continues to stick together for the sake of their children, family and society. (This is quite possible and its probability may be more than the first two cases.)
4. Love does not happen at all, but the couple stays together forever. (The probability of this is the highest.)

From my discussions with men and women past their middle age, I can state with conviction that most of them don't have an enjoyable time in bed. A majority of the men complain that their wives have lost interest in sex and that it has been quite a few years since they had a good time together in bed. In most cases, the men end up assuming that their wives have become old and that women who are past middle age simply lose their appetite for sex. Women also tend to find this assumption convenient, though the fact is that most of them (and some of them may not even be aware of this) are just bored and tired of the way sex is handled by their men. Night after night, for years, their husbands and partners have not taken care to make sure sex is enjoyable for them. No wonder women let men think that they are uninterested in sex.

I am reminded here of the famous philosopher Jiddu Krishnamurti, who said, 'A husband never relates with his wife and a wife never relates with her husband. They only relate with the image they have created of the wife or the husband, and this applies to almost all our relationships and not just the spouses.' This holds good a 100 per cent when it comes to sexual relationships.

The truth is that men and women are caught in a vicious trap. While men don't pause to think, even for a moment, if there is any problem in the way they are handling sex or why their wives are not showing an interest in sex, we cannot blame them alone. All along, men have been thinking that their wives are enjoying having sex with them, whereas, in reality, their wives have just been tolerating them, thinking it's their duty to keep the men happy. They have been quiet about their dissatisfaction out of love for their husbands and because they don't want to hurt them by revealing the truth. Under the garb of patni vratham (wifely duties), they've been having sex with their husbands mechanically, not knowing that there are other ways of having sex and enjoying it.

So, for a husband, it is quite natural to assume that his wife's refusal to sleep with him is because she has become old and no longer enjoys sex.

What he should actually be doing instead is changing his thinking and his ways. He should learn to care for his wife's enjoyment. But, as I said earlier, men and women are both caught in a vicious loop.

Frustrated with the lack of sex at home and scared of pursuing an extramarital affair, many men beyond the age of fifty start getting desperate for sex. Thus begin the horrible acts of perversion—brushing against women and standing too close to them in buses, and trying to molest innocent kids. Because sex is always on their mind, these men are unable to control themselves when the slightest opportunity to appease their urge arises.

15

Marriage and Family

LET US UNDERSTAND THAT ALL RELATIONSHIPS are need-based. Marriage too is need-based, considering that most people enter into one for the sake of their convenience and comfort.

Allow me to explain this in detail. As we grow up and watch our parents age, we start thinking of our own old age. We assume that just like we are looking after our parents and supporting them, our children too will take care of us during our old age. We then start thinking of getting married, because if we are not married and if we don't have a family of our own, our lives will become uncertain. We fear we'll be left alone in the world.

If we're already married and have a family, we feel that we have fulfilled the purpose of our life. Attachments and responsibilities in the form of a spouse and children give us a sense of accomplishment. And that is the purpose of marriage.

When you get married, there is someone to take care of your needs; someone who knows what you want and is willing to do that for you. There is someone with whom you can share your happy and sad moments, and create a family with. Most importantly, there is someone readily available to go to when you need to release your sexual energy. All in all, while marriage may look like a great concept that has worked well in the eyes of onlookers, it has not always worked well for everyone. But then, like everything else in life, we've all been taught to accept the institution of marriage as it is. We've been told to compromise, adjust and just be (not live). We've all been instructed to pretend for the sake of society that there is harmony at home, and that the family we have created meets all societal norms and expectations. This is how most couples celebrate their silver jubilee and golden jubilee anniversaries.

But the reality is greatly different. Consider this situation: A man comes home tired after a hard day's work. He is greeted by his wife who has had an equally tough day at home managing everything, from domestic chores to the children. In the evening, when she serves dinner to the family, the man eats it silently. He doesn't think of the toil and labour that has gone into cooking the food. He doesn't appreciate the food because he thinks it's his wife's 'duty' to cook for the family. The woman too doesn't appreciate the hard work the man has put in for them to be able to afford the food they are eating. She thinks earning a living is the man's duty.

As they have their food, the husband and the wife talk about mundane things—how the children are faring in school, what they could become once they grow up, some repair work that needs to be done and so on.

Then, once they are done eating, it is time for them to go to bed, with the woman thinking about what to make for breakfast and the man wondering what file to tackle first in office the next morning.

As far as their sex lives are concerned, if, during the week, the wife wants to have sex, she is very likely to quell that desire because she knows that her husband is too tired and has to go to office in the morning. The weekend would be a better time, she tells herself. The man, on the other hand, will still choose to satisfy his sexual needs even when he is tired or doesn't have enough time.

Please believe me when I tell you that the scene in most Indian bedrooms is not at all like what you see in the movies, with a husband and wife looking at each other with loving eyes or kissing the other's forehead with tenderness and all that. Instead, it is all about quickly removing each other's clothes (sometimes not even that) and jumping into the act straightaway. The man hurriedly does a few push-ups on top of the woman in an urge to relieve himself, and there ends the matter. He'll turn aside and sleep once he's done, while the woman, now completely aroused, will bear a few sleepless hours before she finally dozes off. And the next morning, the man will expect his wife to make him breakfast—that too with love!

When life becomes so monotonous and predictable, the sanctity of marriage is lost. And yet, we still want to get married and have children because that is what is expected of us by society. Living the one life that has been given to us is not as important as completing our life cycle by doing things that others expect us to do. People think that if they stay single, they will get alienated from the crowd. But here's the thing: Even if the crowd were to consist entirely of fools and hypocrites, we'd still think it's important to be one among the crowd!

At this stage in life, however, I strongly believe that not every man and woman's purpose in life is to get married and build a family. People have unique and individual purposes which are independent of the cycles of marriage and family. That said, if we want a happy married life, we have to bring in changes in the way marriage and family are perceived.

What should these changes be?

To begin with, marriage is not a business transaction where we sign a contract, and abide by the terms and conditions. Where a business deal revolves around products and services, a marriage involves people and their feelings. One has to be very clear about this—love is a spontaneous feeling that cannot be imposed on anyone, neither can it arise from the pages of a legal agreement.

In a marriage, people promise their spouses that they will take care of their needs forever and they will always love them. Fortunately, if one stays healthy and wealthy till they die, they can keep their promise. But how can anyone promise to love another person forever? What comes spontaneously can also vanish spontaneously, right?

Traditionally, we've been told that one should not seek love outside marriage. However, in my opinion, this conditioning has to go. If my partner is to be happy in our marriage, then I have to be happy. And vice versa. But for how long can I put on a happy face when my partner is sporting a long one? Things are really as simple as that.

The atmosphere at home has to be happy, and making sure it stays so is in my hands. If my partner has found a new love outside our marriage, I have to let him enjoy that love because that will keep him happy. As a bystander, I should not jump in and ask what is wrong with me and why my partner has fallen in love with someone else? This line of questioning itself is absurd. There need not be anything wrong with me for my husband to fall in love with someone else. On the contrary, this only shows that he has a loving heart and that he can love one more person.

So, if you come to know that your partner or spouse has fallen in love with someone else, just brush it aside and continue to be how you have always been with them. Do not push them into a corner by asking them questions that make them feel guilty about what they are doing. Just ignore everything and simply observe the transformation at home when they come back a happier person. They will be in a better state of mind and they will spread happiness around them. Granted, this will be a very hard thing to do initially, but it will bring the desired effect of creating joy and happiness within your family.

If, however, you react badly to your spouse's new-found love, you will end up forcing them to make a choice—either they leave you or they leave the other person. If they choose you, they will, in all probability, live with you like a walking vegetable. Love will be replaced entirely by bitterness and regret in your relationship. If you love your spouse truly and you want them in your life, you will not force them to make a choice. You will allow them to LIVE and you will also LIVE.

Also, we should not try to measure love or compare it. We should just love, for the sake of love. Your spouse's 'affair' may either go on for some time or it may stop after a while. Whatever happens, you must remain unaffected by it because they continue to remain your spouse. As long as they still care for you, and take care of you and your family, you should be happy. Do not think that just because your spouse now loves someone else, they no longer love you. This is, in truth, an absurd belief. When a second child is born to a couple, do the parents stop loving their first kid? No. Love is not something that is stored in a limited quantity in our hearts. It's not something that can be divided or portioned out. It's not that when we give out love, it gets depleted within us. In fact, the more we love, the more capable we become of loving others and the more it grows in our heart. Love is the only thing that does not diminish with overuse and it's also the only thing that doesn't have any boundaries. We can love anything and everything.

Our greatest mistake is that we live for the sake of society. We want society to respect and admire us. We give more importance to superficial things than living a life of our choice. But remember, if you lose a life of happiness, you become lifeless and then society won't even bother to remember you.

When you don't respect the fellow human being you might be married to, why bother giving respect to lifeless things? This is akin to making a mockery of the whole system.

If your marriage is a success, talk about it. Let people around you learn how to make a marriage work. If your marriage is a failure, then too you must talk about it. Let people around you know why a marriage fails.

16

Possessiveness

Love gives naught but itself and takes naught but from itself, love possesses not nor would it be possessed: For love is sufficient unto love.
—Kahlil Gibran, *The Prophet*

If our love is only a will to possess, it is not love.
—Thich Nhat Hanh, *Peace Is Every Step: The Path of Mindfulness in Everyday Life*

Mine. The language of love is like that, possessive. That should be the first warning that it's not going to encourage anyone's betterment.
— Holly Black, *Black Heart*

HAVEN'T WE ALL HEARD SOMEONE OR THE other say to their partner, 'You are mine'? There is a lot of possessives that is evident in that statement and the one who is the subject of this statement often feels proud on hearing it. But what is there to be proud of in this situation? How can someone become 'ours'? Even the children we give birth to are not ours. They are separate individuals. However, in the name of love, we always end up trying to possess the other person, because we want to ensure they are stuck with us for life.

Only lifeless objects can be possessed. When the object of our love is another life, it needs space and air to grow and blossom.

Osho narrates a small story to make us understand how possessiveness is evil, and how it destroys both love and the object of our attachment.

A nun, in search of enlightenment, made a wooden statue of the Buddha and covered it with a gold leaf. It was a very pretty statue and she carried it with her wherever she went.

The Toilet Seat

Years passed and the nun finally settled down in a small country temple where there were many statues of the Buddha, each with its own shrine. Every day, the nun would burn incense before her golden Buddha. But she didn't want the fragrance of her incense sticks to stray on to the other statues. So, she devised a funnel through which the smoke would ascend to her shrine alone. Happy with this arrangement, the nun continued with her worship. But what she didn't realize was that this actually blackened the nose of her beloved golden statue and made it ugly.

This is what happens to a relationship when possessiveness becomes a part of it—ugliness sets in and ruins the relationship.

If we don't love ourselves, we cannot love anyone else. But if we do love ourselves, we will not want to spoil our peace, and if we don't want to spoil our peace, we must go beyond distrust, doubts and possessiveness, and simply be 'one' with the person we love. Love is beautiful; why would any sane and rational person want to turn away from that beauty?

The truth is that for a doubting eye, even water appears to be a mirage. Many a times, it's the strength of a particular doubt that makes it appear true.

Mostly, our possessiveness concerns the body of the person we claim to love. No one's mind or heart is visible to our naked eyes. So, we concentrate on the other person's physicality, forgetting that in all our efforts to possess the other person, we can only possess their body, and not their hearts and minds. The more the body is chained, the more the heart longs for freedom and the mind starts working on achieving this freedom. In the process, we not only lose the person in entirety, but we also get increasingly possessed by our own malevolent thoughts.

Why do we even try to possess people as though they are goods bought by us? For heaven's sake, why do we not remember that everyone is an individual in their own right and that no one can be a mirror image of us? Let us give that respect to each other. Let us accept that nothing can be achieved by force but everything can be accomplished with love.

Love is about giving freedom to others and allowing them to live their life. It's about learning to love the other person even when you think the relationship is going to die. Maybe this love will act like a healing medicine, like somras, and keep the relationship alive. Who knows? But possessiveness will only ruin the relationship and, while the marriage may still exist, the people involved will die a slow death.

We have but one life. We should love ourselves and others in it, and not allow ourselves to become trapped in lifeless, loveless relationships.

17

Complementing Each Other

I OFTEN WONDER ABOUT THE DIFFERENCES between a man and a woman—which of these differences are created by nature and which ones are created by human beings? What is the origin of these differences and what is their effect on our lives?

Life is a beautiful thing arising from the fusion of a woman and a man, their union creating generation after generation of human beings. This union brings forth joy and wealth in the universe of nature. It is such a lovely feeling to hold a tiny being in one's arms—an innocent creature born out of the efforts of two people.

What is more beautiful is the entire process that leads to the birth of a new life into this world. It is so interesting, so pleasurable for the two people involved in it. We owe our thanks to nature for having made it all possible—otherwise you and I wouldn't be here today.

Nature has created men and women in such a way that they are interdependent for their survival. This interdependence starts even before birth. To even conceive a foetus—irrespective of the gender the child is born into—both the man and the woman need to come together. The act of reproduction requires both genders. A woman has certain functions in the process and the man has his own. One cannot do without the other. Such are the amazing ways of nature.

By making two human beings in different forms and with different functions come together, nature has ensured that man and woman work in unison towards the growth of their own species. Whatever lacks in a man can be found in a woman and whatever lacks in a woman can be found in a man, for both have been designed in a way that they complement each other.

However, in the name of marriage and family, most people seem to have forgotten this basic fact. They are not living the life they would really love to live. Instead, they have become hypocrites caught in a farce.

In our society, most marriages happen between the ages of 25 to 30 years, and a person ends up spending more time with his or her spouse than they do with their parents. But how many people are truly prepared to understand what it means to complement a partner at this age? How many of them are actually ready to start a family? How many are clear about the kind of responsibilities they are taking on and the sort of roles they need to play with respect to their spouse, children and in-laws? Do they realize that their own family dynamics will change with the start of the new relationship?

When you're old enough to take up the responsibility of a family, shouldn't you also know what awaits you? While there are people who decide that marriage is not their cup of tea and prefer to live alone, they are far and few in between (hats off to these guys!). Most people, however, opt for marriage just to follow the norms of society and because they don't want to be alone, especially in their old age. There are also those who get married just because they are tired of people asking them why they are not married yet or because they don't want the rumour mill to speculate about why they are single. But are these the right reasons to get married?

I wonder why people are such hypocrites when it comes to the question of marriage. Everybody says that marriage is a commitment and, whether you like it or not, once you commit to it, you have to stick to it. Yes, I agree that marriage is a commitment, but what kind of a commitment is it? Is it a commitment to abide by your spouse's rules and regulations at all times, to take care of their needs and sleep with them whenever they want to? Is it a commitment to bear children together? Is it about showing the world outside that the two of you are an 'ideal' couple?

Instead of all this, should we not think of marriage as a commitment to complement the other person in all aspects of life? How many people really consider any of the following as a promise they should make when they enter into a marriage?

- To treat the other person as an equal human being.
- To understand that the other person has their own mind, heart and navel (I read somewhere that the source of life energy comes from the navel and not from the heart.)
- To accept that the other person has the right to 'live' as much as they do.
- To believe that the other person is entitled to as much freedom as they would like to have.
- To acknowledge that the other person has a right to voice their thoughts and views, and that they have to be heard too.
- To appreciate the fact that a decision taken on behalf of the family has to be acceptable to both.

- To understand that the woman who stays home and takes care of the family contributes more to the family than the man who goes out and earns money.
- To understand that the man who goes out to earn money for the family goes through all kinds of mental and physical hardships to keep the family in good stead.
- To accept that the other person is an individual, and needs some time and space to do what they like to do.
- To understand that the other person too has their dreams and ambitions, and that these need to be supported and nurtured.

Above all, people should understand that a husband or wife's role is not limited to the stereotypical tasks of cooking, earning a living, sleeping together or parenting, but that both of them should be willing to play all the roles, as the situation demands. They should be friends at all times—for friendship is the basis on which any good relationship is built. If you look at any successful couple, you will notice that they share a very good friendship between them, one which allows them to be individuals and also partners. They don't imprison each other in the name of 'love'. Their marriage is not a block they are stuck with. They are both living together, breathing deeply and freely, and also living their own lives. The love between them is alive because their hearts are not dead. This is the true meaning of two people complementing each other in every which way.

18

Driving Away Inhibitions

WHEN PARTNERS DON'T OPENLY communicate with each other about their likes and dislikes, it can give rise to a lot of misunderstandings between them, which, in turn, can lead to great dissatisfaction, especially when it comes to their sex lives. One may feel unfit for sex or look at their partner as being sexually inadequate. How then, do we address this problem?

It is taken for granted that people learn how to have sex once they find a partner, but how does one learn about what the other person likes or dislikes?

Imagine cooking for your partner regularly and thinking that they like the food. But what if whatever you cook is actually not to their liking? Or what if you think you can sing, but when you do, it sounds like Greek or Latin to your partner? If you force them to eat your food or listen to you sing every day, they will only be waiting for an opportunity to walk out one day.

What is needed here is clear communication without any inhibitions. Is this dish to your liking? Do you like how I sing? Do I sing well at all? Don't we usually ask such questions to people and take their feedback? Then why this communication gap when it comes to sex?

The problem starts with people considering sex a dirty word and not wanting to talk about it at all—not even with their partner. The act of having sex is fine; we are prepared to do it once we get into bed with our partner. However, we are not prepared to discuss the act itself, especially with our partner. In fact, we may not find it difficult to discuss our sex life with our closest friends, but we are not comfortable doing so with our partner.

What is this strange inhibition? Why can't we accept that sex is an integral part of life and just get rid of the taboo attached to it? What are we afraid of? Are we scared we will erode our value system? But then, value systems have to be tweaked here and there to suit the current environment, isn't it? We cannot argue that just because our ancestors spent a lot of time and energy creating typewriters, we must continue using them and completely ban computers. However, this is what we're doing in the name of preserving traditions that have been passed down by our ancestors.

The truth is we all have a mind and we need not walk blindly down the same path as our forefathers. If we do so, we are depriving ourselves and our future generations of their right to think and be independent individuals. If there is no transformation or change in our thinking from one generation to the other, then there is no growth in any sphere, including in matters of sex. In this situation then, sex, instead of bringing two people together, can become the reason two people separate or drift away from each other.

For instance, because of our inhibitions, most men don't even try to properly arouse the woman during sex; sometimes, they are just not bothered about whether she reaches an orgasm or not. A few are not even aware that a woman can reach an orgasm. The women, on the other hand, often end up thinking that there is something wrong with them physically as they are not able to achieve an orgasm.

In either case, the fact remains that women's vaginas are used as a toilet seat by most men. I will also go so far as to say that even in cases of oral sex, a woman's mouth is used to ensure the man ejaculates, but he doesn't bother to do the same for her.

All of this, however, could be easily avoided if women shed their inhibitions and conditioning, at least gradually, and speak up about their likes and dislikes. They need to realize that unless they do so, they are very likely to die without experiencing the beauty of shared sex, and the ecstasy and relaxation it gives the mind and the body.

Men, on the other hand, have to remember that sex is to be shared and not just snatched from women. They have to be patient with their partners and find out what turns them on. And together, both partners have to understand that equal and open participation will bring about the best sexual experience for them.

Even the gods seem to have said, 'Seek, and thou shall receive!' So how can we expect our partners, who are mere mortals like us, to give us what we desire without our asking for it specifically? We have but one life to live. Why must we cower behind our inhibitions and not enjoy the pleasures of sex with our partners? Perhaps they don't know what we want. But it is as simple as letting them know what we want and then they will give it to us.

19

Male Ego

SOMEHOW, THE MALE EGO HAS ALWAYS BEEN particularly fragile when it comes to sex. When a woman refuses to have sex with a man or when she expresses her dissatisfaction about sex, a man's ego gets majorly hurt.

But if a man can proudly proclaim that he cannot cook (which is a necessary survival skill for both men and women), why can't he accept a shortcoming in his sexual prowess? Why does he behave as if he's been hit below the belt when a woman tries to make him understand that he is not satisfying her sexually? Why does he behave as if the woman's sole intention was to hurt him? Why does he react so badly?

Instead of taking this as an insult, one can always be sportive, and find ways to make himself better in bed and satisfy his partner, which would do both of them a world of good.

Why should sex be associated with manliness and ego? Sex is something that both partners should enjoy. Both men and women have a part to play in sex, and only when they both play their parts properly can they enjoy being together and coming together. If I'm not doing something properly, I need to know about it. I need to know what gives my partner pleasure. Similarly, I too have certain needs. And if I tell my partner about these needs, then he should listen to me patiently and give me that pleasure.

Why should so normal a thing be allowed to hit a person's ego? Why can't men (or women, for that matter) change their ways to suit the needs of their partner? When the man is willing to understand a woman's needs and show her that he cares about her pleasure, the woman will be willing to do more. This will definitely bring them both closer, not just physically but otherwise too. Won't this make the whole act playful and passionate? What is your problem, man? You say that it's difficult to understand women. But you guys have always puzzled me when it comes to sex.

20

Health and Sex Education

EVERY BOY AND GIRL SHOULD KNOW WHAT they are getting into before they have sex. But how many of us are bothered about our children learning the nuances of sex before they actually engage in the act?

Sex, in my opinion, should be taught to everyone as a science of the body—one that deals with a biological need. Everyone should learn about the chemical and emotional reactions that accompany sex. This understanding will do a lot of good for our youngsters as it will help them maintain a healthy balance between their emotional and physical needs.

If, however, you find it difficult to openly talk about such things with your children, you can look at other options. For example, you can get your children a reliable book about sexual health when they are in their teens.

If you find it hard to give them such books directly, then leave the books in places where you know your children will find them. Every teenager is intrigued by the word 'sex'. So, they are more than likely to pick up the book stealthily (unless they are confident enough to do so in front of you), quietly tiptoe to their room and start reading it. This could be a great way to prepare teenagers for a healthy sexual relationship when the time comes because books on sexual health provide them with a clear understanding of what sex is. This knowledge will prevent your children from having sex prematurely.

Let teenagers equip themselves with the right knowledge so that they can cement their sexual relationships in a proper way as young adults.

The union of two people cannot continue to be a miracle for long. The two people involved in the relationship have to work hard to make things work and, for that, they definitely need to know about sex. Ironically, our social and matrimonial systems always assumes that once two complete strangers get married and start living together, they will have a good sexual relationship and will be with each other until the end of their lives. This incorrect assumption has always been a mystery to me.

Marriages are not made in heaven and there are no angels taking care of the partners. Marriages are arranged and fixed on earth, and the people getting married definitely need to understand each other's wants and desires for them to be truly together. Let us not get carried away by fantasies or old tales. Instead, we need to educate our children about sex and help them navigate its complexities better.

21

Food and Sex

Sex is as important as eating or drinking and we ought to allow the one appetite to be satisfied with as little restraint or false modesty as the other.
—Marquis de Sade

WOULD YOU EVER WANT TO EAT A BOWL OF plain rice, or a few idlis or slices of bread without any toppings or side dishes? Wouldn't you want at least some salt and some spices to up the taste? And even if you eat the rice or the idlis or bread, would you do so without complaining about it at all?

Sex and food are quite alike. They both provide us with sensual pleasure and they both satisfy our hunger. When we don't deprive ourselves of tasty food, even though we know that the bowl of plain rice is enough to fill our stomachs, then why do we deprive ourselves of taste and pleasure when it comes to sex? When an organ as small as the tongue can long for so much sensory satisfaction, why should the body not demand sensual pleasure?

Think about your partner consuming that bowl of plain rice. Will you be able to watch them eat so bland a meal without offering them something to go along with it?

For that matter, when we are deciding what food to make for a family meal, don't we take into account the tastes and preferences of our family members? Don't we try to make food that they will relish? Why do we do so? Is it not to keep them happy and satisfied? To ensure that our family is a successful example of this social institution?

Ideally, we should apply the same logic in the case of sex as well, for it will ensure the success of a marriage, and also keep the relationship between a husband and a wife intact. But this is precisely what we don't do. Instead, we deprive ourselves and our partners of pleasure and satisfaction simply because we don't want to talk about sex. This is how deep our conditioning is.

If all a man wants is a hole to relieve himself in, he may as well consider an actual toilet seat instead of troubling a woman for sex. And the woman, well, she is better off satisfying herself by masturbating rather than get used as a toilet seat.

22

Loss of Interest in Sex in Women

THOUGH SEX IS A BASIC PHYSICAL NEED, IT HAS to start from the mind for one to enjoy it completely because only when there is a fusion of the mind and the body, does sex give us absolute joy. However, in our society, sex is treated as a physical act alone, one in which only the body is in focus—the mind gets dissolved in the acid that is the 'final act'.

When a man is courting a woman, she is made to believe that he finds beauty in her in many different ways. She is told that her eyes are beautiful and attractive, and that she has a gorgeous body. The attraction between the man and the woman starts with the glances they exchange. The woman enjoys the way the man looks at her, the way he touches her, with even an accidental brushing of their hands sending an electric shock throughout her body. But given the constraints that our society places on a courting couple, all that the woman receives during this period are a few stray caresses from the man. These get registered in her mind as moments of pleasure and her body reacts to them. She longs for closeness and completeness with her man.

However, as far as the man is concerned, once he has intercourse with the woman, he realizes that the act of sex is where his body experiences the maximum enjoyment, ending with him ejaculating. So, every time he gets together with the woman, his focus is only on having intercourse with her. He becomes self-centred and, either knowingly or unknowingly, he begins to believe that it's the same for the woman too. He forgets all about her beautiful eyes and her beautiful body, because all he wants is to insert himself in her hole for a minute or two.

What I don't understand here is this: If a man needs just a woman's vagina for sexual enjoyment, why does he look for women with the supposedly perfect shape? If he is not going to enjoy her entire body, then why impose any beauty standards on women at all? A woman's body is to arouse a man and, once he is aroused, he becomes blind to the woman's needs. He doesn't see her as an individual who is looking forward to his touch and adoration. He forgets that there are things that can arouse a woman as well.

When this is how sex is perceived and engaged in in our conservative society, how can anyone, especially men, expect women to have an active interest in sex for long? Why do men think that women will be happy to sleep with them when the act of sex brings not even the slightest bit of pleasure to them?

23

Value Systems

THIS PHRASE HAS NEVER FAILED TO PUZZLE ME: 'Value systems'. What are these value systems? Who created them? And why? Why are we reluctant to let go of those values which do not bring any benefit to our lives and, instead, adopt new ones that enhance the quality of our lives?

Society creates a lot of drama around these value systems, which are, in truth, not permanent.

I have a friend who was brought up in a village, and wasn't educated. She got married to someone from the city and, after their wedding, she moved to the city.

One day, much to my shock and surprise, she told me that she found some of the city dwellers to be more narrow-minded than the people from her village. To support her statement, she narrated the story of two families from her village. Let me recount them both for you.

In the first story, a teenage girl fell in love with a boy from a different caste. Fearing the wrath of their elders, the two of them ran away to the city and started living together. After a few months, however, the boy ditched the girl and fled to some other place. Not knowing what else to do, the girl went back to her village to ask for her parents' help and forgiveness. Needless to say, the parents were furious. They shouted at her and beat her up as well, but, eventually, they took her back. After a month or so, the girl found out that she was pregnant and that it was well past the safe window for an abortion. Her parents didn't know what to do. So, the whole village gathered and decided that they would find a solution to the problem. In the end, they asked if anyone would come forward to marry the girl, and take care of her and her child as his own family. Seeing her plight, a boy stepped forward and agreed to marry her. 'They are now married and living together rather happily,' my friend said.

What was surprising about this entire situation was that although the entire village knew who the girl had eloped with and whose child it was that she was carrying, the villagers didn't care. Their only concern was the well-being of the girl and her unborn child. They didn't blame fate for what had happened, and they didn't let her life be ruined just because she had committed a mistake. The girl's parents didn't keep her pregnancy a secret; neither did they nor the whole village abandon her.

And the boy who married her and accepted her child as his own did so without bothering about the people around him.

The second story that my friend narrated was about a couple with four children. The family lived in utter poverty, even though the man tried his best to earn a living. He was not very smart, and found it difficult to make both ends meet. His wife had also started doing some odd jobs here and there to supplement the family's income. Even then, both of them struggled to run their household. Then, all of a sudden, the man lost his job and was unable to find another one. Burdened by his family's plight and feeling guilty about his incapability to provide for them, he died by suicide.

A month after the man's death, the people of his village asked his unmarried younger brother if he was prepared to take care of his widowed sister-in-law and her children. They also asked the woman if she was willing to accept the proposal of a matrimonial alliance with her brother-in-law. When they both consented to this, they were allowed to live together. Years have passed since then, and, today, their daughters are married, they have built a house for themselves and they are living together peacefully.

In this village, people clearly didn't think about the financial well-being and moral support alone that a marriage can give, but they also thought about the need to appease one's sexual urges. If the women are left alone, what would they do? How would they manage without a man in their life? This is one of the main reasons for the villagers to take such decisions.

'I've never heard of such things happening in the city,' my friend told me.

It is true that while these things may happen in cities as well, they are not the norm. Such decisions are not taken by the parents or elders of the concerned person; rather, they are taken by the person themself. It may sound all the more better because here control over the decision-making process rests with the affected persons themselves. However, instead of getting any familial or social support for their decisions, the affected people are criticized and ridiculed.

As a society, we're all so caught up in our value systems that we've lost focus of the things that are actually important in our lives. Whether it's in a village or a city, if a girl has sex before marriage, she tends to hide it from everyone because she feels it would bring dishonour to her family. Her parents, if and when they find out about this, also hide it from everyone and quickly get the girl married off. They hide their daughter's 'past' from the bridegroom and his family, preferring instead to carry a burden of guilt throughout their lives. And even though she could possibly get past everything that has happened and try living a peaceful life with her husband, the girl feels burdened by her past and lives a life of eternal gratefulness to her husband.

While I do respect our ancestors for having introduced some discipline into the way we live our lives, I believe that values have been twisted and tweaked here and there, and now and then, to suit people who have control over others, all for their own selfish benefits.

Value systems should exist for the benefit of the people; they cannot be valued greater than the people's life itself.

24

Rules for a Good Relationship

I UNDERSTAND THAT I MAY COME ACROSS AS someone who advocates free sex and affairs outside a marriage without any guilt or care. But that is definitely not the case. If a man and a woman love each other and share a great sexual relationship, they don't normally tend to look at anyone else. Though this would be the ideal way to live, this is not what happens in most relationships.

However, there are, in my opinion, certain rules that must be followed at all times. When I say rules,

I mean unwritten, unspoken rules that prescribe heartfelt care and respect for the other person. These rules will strengthen the relationship between a man and a woman. Following them will ensure that the sex between them will be an exchange of love and that it will bring pleasure for both of them, and not just one person. Let's take a look at these rules:

1. Irrespective of the kind of relationship, couples who're not looking to become parents, should always use contraceptive devices during sex. Please don't ignore this as something trivial. Whether a man uses a condom or not plays a major role in a woman's estimation of him. I've heard (and I don't know how correct this is) that many men don't like to wear a condom while having sex as it doesn't give them complete pleasure. While I empathize with the men, should they not think of the women who experience the constant fear of getting pregnant? If, while having sex, a woman suddenly starts fretting that she may end up becoming pregnant because the man is not wearing a condom, can she enjoy the sex completely? When her mind is struck with fear, will she be completely alive to savour being with the man? The wholesome participation of two people is a must for sustaining a long-standing relationship. A man who doesn't care enough to

prevent a woman from feeling this way will be seen as a self-centred person and he may soon lose the woman's respect.

2. If a woman's periods are delayed, she's very likely to be mentally stressed about it because it can be an indication of her being pregnant. A man must not negate this feeling and act like he is not a part of what she's going through. Instead, he must support her in every way possible. If the woman decides to visit a doctor, he must also accompany her. Just because it doesn't affect him physically, if the man doesn't get genuinely involved in the situation, the woman will be forced to think that he's with her only for the use of her body and is not bothered about her otherwise.

3. The man and the woman must both learn to allow each other the space required. It's very important to understand and accept the other person's nature, and not try to mould them according to our own preferences.

4. While love and care are important, respecting the other person is a basic requirement for any relationship to grow stronger with every passing day. The respect that you show your partner adds a sense of wellness and confidence to the relationship, and makes your partner look forward to nurturing your bond.

5. In a marital relationship, please don't take your spouse for granted under any circumstances.
6. Before making sexual advances on your partner, it's necessary to ensure that they are actually in the mood to have sex at that particular moment. Sometimes, it may just happen that they are desperate to only get emotionally and mentally close to you to gain strength and feel reassured by your presence in their life. They may just want to know that there is someone for them in their time of need. They may simply want to sit and talk about something of importance or something that is troubling them. Let us not always assume that everything will be resolved if you try to change your partner's mood by making a sexual advance. Sex is not always a good diversion. Sometimes, it can actually worsen the situation and there is every chance of you getting branded as an insensitive person who is only concerned about appeasing your sexual wants.
7. Getting into live-in relationships is becoming very common among youngsters today. However, this calls for a great deal of maturity on the part of both people involved. First and foremost, both the man and the woman should keep in mind that the design of a live-in relationship is such that there is no sense of permanency attached

to it. There is, therefore, no point crying about things when and if the relationship ends. Both people should have the maturity not to blame the other person when they decide to walk out, even if it leaves a deep ache in their hearts. Emotions are but emotions, and while we may not have control over them, we can control how we respond to them.

8. If a person is involved in an extramarital relationship, they need to be extra careful about how they handle it. Mostly, extramarital affairs function as a filler for some void or the other that the marriage itself is not able to fulfil. It is important to remember this. The people engaged in the affair should have a complete understanding of the other person's roles and responsibilities towards their family. They should know when to be in touch with them and when to stay away. Just one message sent at the wrong time can land the other person in trouble and wreak havoc in their family's life. If there is genuine love and affection between the people involved, then every care must be taken to not ruin their marriage and their family.

9. Never try to control or keep an eye on everything that your spouse or partner is into. Just live your life—find your own personal pleasures,

spend time with yourself or with your friends and relatives, and don't cling to one person all the time. Being clingy and overbearing will ultimately kill the relationship.
10. Last, but not the least, go beyond trust. Love and respect the person you are with, and allow them to be what they are and what they want to be. This will truly keep your relationship alive till the day you die.

25

A Glimpse into Married Life

I KNOW OF A COUPLE, WELL IN THEIR SEVENTIES, who, in everyone's opinion, are literally made for each other. In fact, there are women who are quite envious of how devoted the husband appears to be to his wife.

I've been visiting this couple since my childhood days because they are my friend's parents and they treat me like their own daughter.

The woman suffers from all sorts of age-related ailments like diabetes, high blood pressure and arthritis. She's been advised to take a walk every day for about ten to fifteen minutes and has a lot of medicines prescribed to her. Her husband, unlike her, is quite hale and healthy, and he has made it a point to take her out for a walk every day.

During my visits to their home, I've seen her husband taking good care of her. He'd often stand with a glass of water in one hand and her tablets in the other, coaxing her to take the medicines on time.

One day, I heard that the woman had had a fall while out on her daily evening walk. I immediately rushed to visit her. As we sat talking, I decided to ask for their views on the topics of sex and marriage as I was in the process of researching this book. I told them about a recently married couple who was already regretting their marriage and then asked them, 'Marriage is fine, it's a convenient concept, but what if the couple is not able to share enjoyable sex with each other? What will they do, as they are stuck with each other for the rest of their life?'

Despite the physical pain she was in, the woman immediately blurted out, 'Whatever happened to me, that's what will happen to everyone else in a similar situation.'

I looked at her in surprise. Her face showed all her pent-up feelings clearly, and I was seriously taken aback. At that age, and after so many years of being married, if she could complain about sexual dissatisfaction, that too in front of her husband, I could only imagine how much she must've been mentally and physically affected because of being sexually starved.

After a while, when the husband went into the kitchen to make coffee for all of us, the woman turned to me and said, 'You think he's actually bothered about my pain or something? Yes, he took me to the doctor, got me the injections and the medicines, but not once in these three days since I fell has he asked me how I am feeling or if my pain has subsided.

'There is absolutely no emotional involvement on his part. The whole world is jealous of me for having a husband like him because it looks like he really cares about me and looks after me, but I alone know what I've been going through. He has never been interested in anything that I was interested in, forget about sex. When I watch a music show on TV, he says it's noisy. He expects me to switch the TV off. If I don't, he retreats to the bedroom and feigns sleep. We are the only two people living here in this house, but he doesn't even spend ten minutes sitting and talking with me. He's either with his books or he's sleeping or doing some household work. I have no one to talk to. Yes, he gives me all the material comforts that one could ask for, but I feel lonely. Do you know that I've never been able to cook anything that I've wanted to eat? Till date, I've only cooked food that he likes to eat.'

'I am sure Uncle won't object to you cooking what you like as long as he gets what he wants as well,' I argued.

'Yes, true, but I cannot cook what he likes and also what I like for every meal. As it is, I spend most of my time in the kitchen. Can you imagine how much longer I would have to stay in the kitchen if I were to do this? I have sacrificed so much to keep him happy, but no one knows about that. For the outside world, everything may seem very rosy in my life, but only I know what is actually happening inside.'

This then, is what a so-called successful marriage looks like from the inside.

But who is at fault here and where is the problem? Is our life so cheap that we allow ourselves to waste it like this? Do we want to end up regretting our entire life while on our deathbed? Unless we live a complete and wholesome life, I'm sure we won't be able to embrace death with both hands outstretched and let go of this world with the satisfaction of having 'lived' our life truly.

26

Child's Play

AT SOME POINT IN TIME OR THE OTHER, almost all of us would've seen children getting together and playing 'kitchen'. You may have done it yourself as a child. It's a very common game, after all. Children don't even know how food is cooked. All they know are a few ingredients like rice, daal, wheat and some vegetables, like potatoes, perhaps. They gather all these in small quantities and start 'cooking' in their tiny toy utensils. They get so engrossed in this activity that they lose track of time. They are also not bothered about the end result; they are just happy 'cooking' the whole day. At the end of it, they may be completely exhausted, but, given a chance, they would probably repeat the game again and again with the same level of vigour and enjoyment.

Sex has to be like this. If one can engage in sex with all the happiness, energy and involvement that can be mustered, then there can never be any boredom. But alas! We all take sex too seriously because we're bothered about the end result—the orgasm, and, in most cases, only one person's orgasm—and we forget about the beauty of the process.

Beautiful sex is where we forget that one person is male and the other is female, and are not bothered about what our particular roles are. Sex has to be enjoyed in a complete state of bliss, without any concerns about gender and expected gender roles. Just like the children, all sitting and cooking together, sex too must be a fun act where everyone does everything and participates fully.

We must play in such a way that it gives pleasure to the soul and that pleasure can then transcend into the body as well. Have we ever thought of sex as an act that can give pleasure and comfort to the soul? It's actually strange that we don't think of it this way. When we have sex with someone we love, we're with a person with whom we have no secrets, there is no shame between us. A body that clothes itself in front of others and makes sure that its private parts are not seen or touched by others, experiences absolute freedom during sex. It becomes shameless and takes pleasure in seeing and touching the person's body. This shared shamelessness is liberating and the body's nakedness is a personification of the soul's nakedness, which allows us to become one.

27

Myths about Love and Sex

LET ME DEBUNK SOME MYTHS SURROUNDING love and sex:
1. *Love is tied to social standing, looks and beauty.* We are often confronted by questions like: 'What am I lacking that you cannot love me?' 'Am I not good-looking?' 'Am I not educated?' 'Am I not earning well?' 'What have you found in the other person that I don't possess?

    In truth, love is beyond all this. One cannot explain in so many words why we get attracted to one particular person and not the other.

Remember, no one is inferior or superior in matters of love. We are all equal. It is just that love is an emotion that arises naturally.

2. *Great physical sex in bed can also be emotionally satisfying.* No, only when sex forms a great emotional connection between the two people involved can it be both sexually and emotionally satisfying.

3. *Women lose interest in sex once they hit menopause because of the changes their bodies go through.* On the contrary, with age comes an understanding of what we like and what we don't. An understanding and energetic partner can always keep the woman interested in sex, irrespective of her age.

4. *When a man or a woman has another partner, their love for their spouse vanishes.* This is an assumption that is based on a very limited understanding of love. In a situation like this, it's best to just leave your spouse alone and not ask any embarrassing questions. You must believe that your partner still loves you more than anyone else in the world.

5. *If a person is not possessive about their spouse or partner, then they actually don't love them and are indifferent to them.* No, we can only possess lifeless things, not people. A heart that is full of life can

only love when it is allowed the full freedom to do so.
6. *Only a man gets aroused by certain parts of a woman's body.* Well, certain parts of a man's body can arouse the woman too. You see, it's all in the mind and both the genders have minds.

28

A Conformist View

Having talked at length about sex and the way it has become a dirty, twisted thing, let me finally move from my rather liberal views on the matter to the more conformist view of sex within marriage.

Marriage and sex within a marriage are actually beautiful and well-thought-out concepts. But somewhere down the line, we've missed out on the basics required to make these concepts work for both the people involved in a marriage.

We acquire many friends throughout our lifetime. Every friendship is the outcome of a choice we make to be with the other person. And in every friendship, there is a common thread connecting the two friends. This common thread is made up of common interests. It could be anything—from playing a particular sport and listening to a certain genre of music to travelling together. It could be something very small, but always, this common thread gives them pleasure and keeps their life interesting. It acts as a bridge between the two friends, and although they themselves may not have thought about it, this is how it happens.

I wonder how many people look for common interests in a marriage, irrespective of whether it's an arranged marriage or a love marriage. Generally, people consider things such as physical attraction, societal status, family background, education, etc.—and it's not entirely wrong to look at these things. But along with these, one must also look for common interests.

Any relationship will be interesting until the time we explore each other completely. It could take a few months or a few years, but one fine day, when we know everything about the other person, our interest in them will vanish, and we will begin to take them for granted and vice versa. Then comes monotony. We go to office, we keep the house clean, we take care of the children and we plan for their future. That's it. There are people

The Toilet Seat

who make the effort to keep their life interesting and make their marriage work. These efforts include making compromises, which means that they do things that they wouldn't normally like to do. But for how long can a person keep doing things that they don't want to do, simply for the sake of keeping the other person happy? Aren't we losing our lives in the process?

Think of this situation: A man is crazy about rock music while his wife loves listening to melodious songs in a peaceful atmosphere. When the husband switches on his favourite tracks, the whole house reverberates with rock music. What does the woman do? She just waits for when her husband goes out for a while so that she can listen to her melodies in peace. Or it could be the other way around as well.

Basically, the dominant person enjoys their life, while the submissive one waits for an opportunity to do what they love to do.

Let us take another example: The husband prefers to confine himself to a comfortable air-conditioned room to take a break from his daily routine, while the wife prefers to walk amidst nature in order to relax. For each of them to enjoy a short respite from their everyday lives then, they both have to be alone. The man will take his break inside a room and the woman will take hers outside in a park. This will slowly but surely result in them breaking up.

If a husband and a wife cannot share a break and spend joyful moments together, then what is the point of a marriage which expects two people to be partners for life? In the eyes of society, theirs might be a successful marriage as long as they live under the same roof, but, in reality, their lives are a failure.

When two people have common interests (in at least six out of ten things), there's no need to make an extra effort to keep the relationship interesting. When they are together, they can enjoy doing these common things. They can hold each other's hands and take a walk amidst nature. They can listen to rock music and head bang. They can explore a Chinese restaurant that might have recently opened up in their locality. The remaining four things where their tastes differ can be done when they are alone. This is a real partnership, where one doesn't have to wait for the other person to go out so that they can enjoy what they want to do!

Not many of us think about these things before deciding to get married. But that doesn't mean it's impossible to understand and appreciate our partner's interests after marriage. We can think of these interests like an 'acquired taste'. One could begin by trying to understand what makes a particular activity or thing interesting for their partner. See if that is something that can be learned. For all you know, with time, it could become something that you love to do as well! All it takes is a little bit of flexibility and openness of mind to keep a relationship interesting and make things work.

Deriving enjoyment from sex also depends on how good we are at making the other person enjoy it. Let's suppose that both the people in a relationship love potatoes. But if one likes it fried and the other likes it boiled, there could be a problem. The solution to this would be to fry the potatoes on some days and boil them on others. This way, both people get what they want and a balance is struck. Sex is also like that. A couple must be able to give in to each other's interests and preferences so that, at the end of the day, the sex is not taken for granted and both of them derive happiness out of it.

Granted that sex is very important, but it's equally important to acknowledge the fact that two people cannot keep having sex all the time. It cannot be the only thing that keeps them together (and if that is, in fact, the case, then it's a rather pathetic relationship). Spending quality time with each other also matters a lot. And the time a couple spends together can be called 'quality time' only if both of them truly enjoy doing certain things together, without having to make a conscious and deliberate effort to keep the other person happy. This would naturally bring them happiness because they would both be doing what they like, with the person they like. Only then can their relationship survive; otherwise, it's the institution of 'marriage' that continues to live, not the people involved.

29

Need of the Hour and Hope for the Future

WE HAVE A LOT TO LEARN AND UNDERSTAND if we are to change things by raising our kids right, for there is no one else who can guide our children along the right path. As long as we are not able to eradicate the offences, we must keep building up defences. We must also create an awareness among all adults about teaching and actively demonstrating before young boys the need to respect women both at home and at large. And sex has to be taken out of the closet and made a part of healthy conversations with kids, so that the myths surrounding it are all addressed and their doubts are cleared.

If this transition happens in our male-dominated, women-objectifying society, we can hope to see some positive changes in the way sex is perceived and handled. Maybe, a day will come when men and women will enjoy a great union of the mind and the body when they have sex. We will then become oblivious to gender differences in the pure pleasure of our soul.

Here, I quote one of the women who responded to Nancy Friday's call for women to share their sexual fantasies for her book *The Secret Garden*:

> I don't pretend to know what makes people work, but I'd be willing to bet that if more people were more open and let themselves go during sex, their brains as well as their bodies, the world would be a better place. I doubt if so many people would be so aggressive and power-crazy if they found a suitable sex partner who would accept all of them. If people could free themselves of deep-rooted sex guilt, they'd spend more time becoming good lovers, and wouldn't have so much time for revenge and wars. Good sex makes my husband and me very mellow.

Who would think of hating and fighting and plotting to get someone else if they'd just been very sexually satisfied, no matter what means they employed to reach that happy goal? Not many, I'll bet.

Sex has become unnecessarily complicated when, in reality, it needs to be talked about at length, considering it's a part and parcel of every individual's life. We need more dialogue and debates around it to make it simple (or maybe even make it more complicated!).

I don't expect everyone who has read this book to agree with all the points I've made. The views expressed in this book are, as Wordsworth describes his poetry, 'the spontaneous overflow of powerful feelings' of mine.

But if this book triggers even a single mind to ponder over the questions raised, I'd be very happy to have achieved the purpose of writing this book.

Thank you, once again, for having picked up *The Toilet Seat*. I wish you an enjoyable journey through life.

Love,
Latha

Addenda

*(Afterthoughts that cropped up after
the first edition of the book)*

30

Is There an Upper Age Limit for Sex?

THE IDEA THAT MENOPAUSE MARKS THE END OF a woman's sexual urges has been widely ingrained into both men and women's minds. However, what it marks is simply the end of a woman's fertility—in other words, her ability to have children.

So deep-rooted is this conditioning that even when a menopausal or post-menopausal woman feels sexually aroused, she believes that there's something wrong with her. She's afraid to be open with her husband about this, almost as if it's a crime to have sexual urges at this stage in her life. She quietly assumes that this is only happening to her and that other women are not experiencing such an urge. Shame creeps in and complicates things further.

Even women who are physically and emotionally fit, and who continue to have sex without any hindrance after menopause, tend to believe that they don't actually need sex anymore.

In truth, a woman is prone to be more sexual after her menopause (I heard a psychologist say this!). This could be because by the time she hits this stage, she's no longer hassled by the task of nurturing children, her menstrual cycles have ceased and she isn't worried about becoming pregnant. Now, she has a lot of time to think about herself and concentrate on her own needs.

Menopause is not an overnight development. It's a slow process and a woman may exhibit symptoms of menopause anywhere between a few months to a few years before it actually sets in. Because of the physical and mental changes that come with menopause, it might take a little longer for a woman to get sexually aroused. This is often mistaken as a waning interest in sex. However, an empathetic partner who is attuned to these changes can be physically and emotionally supportive. He can give her the reassurance that despite the changes unfolding inside her body, he will continue to love her and be with her. He can be patient and extra attentive while having sex with her, so that both of them can have passionate and satisfying sex.

What everyone conveniently forgets is the fact that men also go through the ageing process like women. They start showing signs of disintegration as well. Sometimes, for instance, they are not able to get an erection even after trying to stimulate themselves. Or they might end up ejaculating too soon. But people are so foolish that they boast about men needing sex till they land in their graves! Nature, however, is never biased; it treats everyone equally. Women have the same sexual needs as men do; only their emotional and physical health decides whether this sexual need remains till they go to their graves or if it vanishes before that.

But the sad truth is that ours is a society which insists that for a woman, irrespective of her age, sex is not mandatory at all; that her focus should always only be on her family and her children; and that she loses interest in sex after childbirth. By doing so, we've blinded women, and kept them from their own needs, and allowed men to rationalize their search for sex outside marriage.

Menopause is common to both genders. Maybe the stage at which it comes and the ways it manifests are different for men and women. But men and women are only different physically to enable reproduction. All other differences have been conceived of and spread by selfish people. Men should understand that all these misconceptions affect not only women, but them as well. Only if both partners understand and empathize with each other will their relationship become more wholesome and beautiful.

31

Role of Parents in Child Sexual Abuse

NOT A SINGLE DAY PASSES WITHOUT THERE being some news or the other about a child being sexually abused. These stories make our blood boil. We rant and rave about the punishments not being severe enough to deter the perpetrators. We rue over why such things keep happening all the time. But who is actually responsible for these crimes? US! Yes, us, the ones talking aggressively about all this. We, as individuals and as a society, are responsible for these horrific crimes.

It is our inability to properly understand sex that has created this situation in society. Raising every boy to be a male chauvinist and every girl as an unwanted, second-class citizen is the biggest blunder every parent makes. Add to this the fact that most parents don't help their child acquire an understanding about sex when they are twelve or thirteen years of age. Research also shows very clearly that in most instances of child sexual abuse, the perpetrator is a person close to the child's family. So, the inability to create a safe and secure atmosphere at home is also the result of every parent's carelessness!

Of course, a child can get sexually abused outside of home as well. Such things can happen anywhere—when the kid is playing in a park, at school or when it steps out on its own. But these can be considered accidents, because until and unless every individual changes, there is no way that the world outside can become a safe place for all. And complete societal change cannot happen overnight.

However, as parents, it's our primary responsibility to ensure that such abuse is not inflicted on our kids inside our homes and other supposedly safe places, by people around us who mask themselves as 'good people'. If we cannot create the right atmosphere where our children can feel safe and be at peace, then who else can do it?

The Toilet Seat

Consider the following scenario: A one- or two-year-old toddler is picked up by a visiting relative. The toddler had been joyfully playing and crawling around until then. But now, it suddenly starts crying. How many parents, in a situation like this, will tell the visitor to please leave the child alone? On the contrary, they will tell the kid to stop crying. 'This is your uncle,' or 'This is your grandpa,' they will say as they try to pacify the kid and coax it to accept the person. Never do we, as adults, stop for a minute to think whether or not we are doing the right thing. Never do we consider the kid's feelings or the fact that we could be forcing it into something that it detests.

Up until a certain age, children live by their own instincts! If, as in the above example, an otherwise happy kid cries when it's picked up and held by another person, then it means that it doesn't want to be near that person; it has taken an instinctive dislike to that person. When we force the kid to go against its instincts, we are actually making it lose its trust in us. The kid will no longer see us as protectors. Its confidence in the parents breaks into pieces!

In most instances, as children grow, they start believing that their parents are not on their side; that for them, the outsider or the third person is always more important than they are. This loss of trust in the parents is the reason why 90 per cent of children don't open up to their parents about sexual harassment or any other unwanted incident that might have happened to them.

There is also absolutely no need to teach children about good touch, bad touch and all that. I know this is a rather controversial stand to have right now. But such teachings will only force the children to analyse every single touch and interaction. It will make them confused, and afraid of everything and everyone. Kids have a natural and innate ability to feel all this. Their instincts are strong until we corrupt them with our foolish beliefs. Haven't we all witnessed children showing an aversion to getting physically close with certain people? When these people try to pull the kids close to them, they try to slip out of their hold. This is their instinct kicking in. Instead of reprimanding our kids in such situations, we should tell the person straightaway to not disturb the kid. That is our foremost duty and that is how we manifest our love towards the kid.

We can always talk to the kids once the visitors have left and try to understand why they behaved the way they did. Just because we may respect that person and think nicely of them doesn't mean we can force our kids to do the same. For all we know, unknown to us, our kids might have seen the person's true colours!

As parents, we must show our children, in both words and deeds, that no one in this world is more important to us than them.

No matter how busy we are, we should take care to find out about even the smallest of changes in their lives. We should let them know that we love them a lot, and that we will treat their mistakes as human errors and not as crimes as horrific as murder. We should never demean them in front of anyone, for it will eventually make them lose their trust in us. And we should always remember that the emotional well-being of our children is deeply affected by our own actions and words. Let us always strive to hold their hands and walk with them as we help them become self-reliant, responsible and mature adults who can start living their lives with self-confidence, peace and freedom.

ACKNOWLEDGEMENTS

I OWE MY THANKS TO ALL THE PEOPLE I HAVE MET and all those who have played a part in my life. These are the people who have inspired me to write this book, directly or unintentionally.

I owe my gratitude to all my dear friends and relatives and a few strangers too. Some of my friends enthusiastically supported me, while there were also others who were not in favour of me writing this book. (Sex remains a taboo topic in our country, and writing about it is not always considered an achievement.) Yet, despite their reservations, even some of the naysayers ended up sharing their experiences and perspectives with me.

ACKNOWLEDGEMENTS

I will fail in my duty if I do not talk about Chandru, the designer of this book's cover. Chandru sat with me for countless hours, making an earnest effort to understand the book, so that the design he created did justice to my work. Thank you, Chandru! Your understanding and dedication gave me a lot of energy and confidence.

Thanks to my sister, Pavithra, the first reader of my manuscript. Thanks for pointing out the repetitions and redundancies, which I am quite known for.

And of course, I must thank my grown-up children who, despite realizing the implications of writing on this subject, in a society like ours, gave me the go-ahead for this book, or rather clearly said that they wouldn't stand in my way of sharing my views in public.

A big thank you to the team at HarperCollins India. The day I received their call expressing interest in publishing my book was one of pure elation. From drafting the contract to editing and finalizing the content, their involvement and support were amazing and made the entire process seamless.

Lastly, I am deeply grateful to you for picking up this book. I sincerely hope it sparks reflection, conversation, and perhaps even a small positive change in the lives of its readers.

Love,
Latha

ABOUT THE AUTHOR

Latha was born and brought up in Chennai, Tamil Nadu, and has been writing poetry since the age of twenty. She has always questioned the validity of many of our social norms and the hypocrisies that are hidden under the garb of tradition and culture—in her family and in society at large, where she witnessed the stealthy and shocking acts of people, which made her realize that appearances are often deceptive.

Driven by the urge to talk her mind out, Latha started publishing a monthly magazine titled *The Way*

Forward, which she used as a medium to voice her views on subjects like religion and education. *The Toilet Seat* is her first book.

HarperCollins *Publishers* India

At HarperCollins India, we believe in telling the best stories and finding the widest readership for our books in every format possible. We started publishing in 1992; a great deal has changed since then, but what has remained constant is the passion with which our authors write their books, the love with which readers receive them, and the sheer joy and excitement that we as publishers feel in being a part of the publishing process.

Over the years, we've had the pleasure of publishing some of the finest writing from the subcontinent and around the world, including several award-winning titles and some of the biggest bestsellers in India's publishing history. But nothing has meant more to us than the fact that millions of people have read the books we published, and that somewhere, a book of ours might have made a difference.

As we look to the future, we go back to that one word—a word which has been a driving force for us all these years.

Read.